CW00537644

THE RAILWAYS OF YORK
A Pictorial Celebration

YORK

Railway Heritage

THE RAILWAYS OF YORK

A Pictorial Celebration

David Mather

Silver Link Publishing Ltd

First published in 2014

British Library Cataloguing in Publication Data

A catalogue record for this book is available from the British Library.

ISBN 978 1 85794 440 2

Silver Link Publishing Ltd
The Trundle
Ringstead Road
Great Addington
Kettering
Northants NN14 4BW

Tel/Fax: 01536 330588
email: sales@nostalgiacollection.com
Website: www.nostalgiacollection.com

Printed and bound in the Czech Republic

Dedication & acknowledgment

For my wife Mair, whose unfailing support and understanding has made this possible.

Special thanks to fellow enthusiast Rick Ward for his invaluable assistance and kind permission to include his images, and those of his late friend Douglas Todd of Seacroft, Leeds.

Front cover: **Preserved Gresley 'A4' 'Pacific' No 60009 *Union of South Africa* leaves York for Edinburgh with 'The Coronation' on 5 July 2008, to celebrate 70 years since the record-setting run of sister loco *Mallard*.**

Frontispiece: **Your author on the footplate of Stanier 'Black 5' at Appleby during the run of 'The Waverley' from York to Carlisle and return on 26 August 2012. *Mair Mather***

Contents

1. Steam days

Yorkshire has a strong claim to be one of the pioneer counties in the development of our railways, and Yorkshire merchants were quick to realise the enormous benefits a railway could bring to their trade. The Leeds & Selby Railway was opened in 1834 to connect with trade operating through Hull Docks, and the subsequent construction of the York & North Midland Railway (Y&NMR) southwards from York in 1839, through Sherburn to Gascoigne Wood, to link with the Leeds & Selby Railway, would soon be extended to join with Lancashire & Yorkshire Railway routes, and south to Doncaster and London. The Great North of England Railway (GNoER) line northwards to Darlington followed in 1841. The Y&NMR reached out to Malton and Scarborough, and to Pickering in 1845, there to connect with the Whitby & Pickering Railway; it was extended to Market Weighton in 1847 and to Knaresborough the following year, before being further extended through Starbeck to Harrogate by the newly formed North Eastern Railway (NER) in 1862. In 1865 the NER extended the Market Weighton branch to Beverley, thereby connecting with the Scarborough-Hull line and completing the York-Hull route. The Foss Islands goods branch was opened by the NER in 1880 and featured a platform dedicated to the Rowntrees chocolate factory, where services for the workforce called until closure in 1988. Finally the Derwent

Valley Light Railway opened its line from York's Layerthorpe station to Cliffe Common near Selby in 1913. Thus York had quickly become an important focal point in a rapidly expanding rail network, with lines serving not only Yorkshire and the North East but also, through various connections, the whole of the country.

The 'old' railway station at York was constructed in 1841, presided over by the City's Lord Mayor, George Hudson, whose ambitious plans for the development of a railway system, bolstered by his free-spending and persuasive style, had led to his being elected as the first Chairman of the newly formed York & North Midland Railway. This was followed by his meteoric rise in power and fortune over the coming decade, as he promoted and sponsored railways throughout the country. However, his reign as the 'Railway King' was to last only until the 1850s, by which time his sometimes dubious methods were coming under increasing scrutiny, and his subsequent fall from grace was rapid, orchestrated largely by none other than his contemporary and successor as York's Lord Mayor, George Leeman. In turn, Leeman would rise to become Chairman of the powerful North Eastern Railway, which took over Hudson's original line, the Y&NMR, in the amalgamation of 1854.

York's station at this time was a terminus with 'dead-end' platforms situated within the City Walls, on the opposite side of the road (the A1036, Queen Street) from the current buildings. Local architect G. T. Andrews (who was later to become a prominent station designer for the Midland Railway) was commissioned to design an arch through the walls to afford access to the buildings within the station. In its early days this proved satisfactory but, as traffic increased over the ensuing decades, the station became more and more cramped as trains had to reverse out of the platforms, or locos had to run round their trains before continuing their journeys.

The potentially chaotic situation was relieved to some degree by the NER's policy of making use of 'ticket platforms' located along the lines just outside the station, before they met to pass through the walls. Here tickets could be checked while the train loco was being detached to run round its train, which might then be propelled into the platform by a pilot loco – a hazardous procedure with frequent mishaps. Also at about this time (the 1860s), additional platforms were constructed at Holgate Bridge, and though these have been sometimes referred to as ticket platforms, this is a misconception, as they were intended for use during York Races and other special events, becoming known locally as the Racecourse Station. These platforms continued in operation until the race meeting held on 24 August 1939, under their correct title of Holgate Extension Platforms. Their buildings were eventually demolished in 1962.

Through the arch in the City Walls part of the platform of the 1841 station can still be seen from Queen Street, though the site is now occupied by offices and car parking spaces.

Above: **Gresley Class 'D49/2' 4-4-0 No 62769 *The Oakley* approaches York from the south, passing the 'Racecourse Station' with an express during 1955. Built at Darlington during December 1934 and shedded first at 50B Leeds Neville Hill and finally at 50E Scarborough, she was withdrawn on 12 September 1958 and cut up at BR's Darlington Works a few weeks later on the 30th.**

Right: **Sister loco No 62772 *The Sinnington* storms past the same location with a train for the south on the same day. Built in January 1935, also at Darlington, her first shed was also Leeds Neville Hill while her final home was 50C Selby. Withdrawn on 24 September 1958, she was cut up on 30 November of that year, also at BR's Darlington Works.**

Right: **Thompson 'B1' 4-6-0 No 61214 eases light engine into York station under Holgate Bridge to resume her duties during 1955. Built by the North British Locomotive Company in Glasgow during July 1947, she was allocated initially to 51E Stockton shed, ending her days at 25F Low Moor (Bradford). Withdrawn on 3 May 1965, she was cut up at Arnott Young's yard at Dinsdale, near Darlington, on 30 June.**

Above: **'Deltic' No 55012 *Crepello* approaches York station from the south, passing Holgate Extension Platforms with a King's Cross-Edinburgh service on 29 September 1979.**

Left: **Passing the site of the Extension Platform at Holgate, with its welcome sign for race-goers, is Inter City 125 HST No 254017 at the head of a train from Edinburgh to London King's Cross, also photographed on 29 September 1979.**

Left: **A small group of onlookers has gathered on the site of what was Holgate Cattle Dock Platform, just under Holgate Bridge, to watch preserved LNER 'V2' No 4771 *Green Arrow* depart from York station with the 'Centenary Express' on 29 August 1979.**

Plans for a new 'through' station at York were sanctioned by Act of Parliament in July 1866, the construction of which would eliminate the troublesome requirement for reversals and run-rounds. The NER's splendid tribute to the Age of Iron, described at the time as 'the finest and largest structure of its kind in the world', was opened in June 1877, complete with an imposing curved roof rising high above the through platforms.

As the importance of York as a railway centre increased following the early years of the Y&NMR, more railway companies began to operate services in and out of the city. In fact, by 1854 the significant operators in addition to the dominant NER were the Midland, Great Northern, Lancashire & Yorkshire, Great Eastern, London & North Western and Great Central companies. Thus the need for servicing facilities became ever more apparent. Consequently, large locomotive sheds were developed at both ends of the new station (York North and York South) together with extensions to the locomotive repair shops originally built by the Y&NMR. York North shed, comprising three 'roundhouses', was completed in 1878; a fourth, complete with coaling stage, was added in 1911. The turntables in these early roundhouses were not capable of handling the largest steam locomotives that began to operate through York in the early 1920s, even though they had been replaced by larger electrically operated versions by 1915; consequently these larger locos had to be turned using the Holgate Junction-North Junction-Clifton Junction triangle. Similarly, the buildings could not accommodate locos such as the latest 'Pacifics', resulting in No 4 shed having to be further upgraded, incorporating a larger 70-foot turntable in place of the previous 60-foot example. The importance of York North shed, with its superior facilities, continued to grow, while that of its 'little sister', South shed, diminished.

Much later, from 1954, the No 1 and 2 roundhouses at York North were demolished to be replaced by a straight shed, while Nos 3 and 4 were rebuilt, though retaining their original turntables. With the demise of steam traction on BR, the roundhouses were closed to steam in 1967 and York's allocation of diesel locomotives were allocated to the straight shed. The two remaining circular sheds were made available to house the new National Railway Museum, completed and opened in 1975, with locomotives gathered around the No 4 shed turntable and coaches around the turntable of No 3 shed. The diesel depot was closed in 1982, when this was also taken over by the Museum, though diesel locos continued to be stabled in the sidings outside. Some of these sidings later became incorporated into the modern traction depot built to service Trans-Pennine Express DMUs, operated by Siemens.

York South shed, which was eventually demolished in 1963, comprised the remains of the old Great North of England Railway's three-road straight shed dating from about 1840 and the NER roundhouse built in 1863. Following their demolition, the site remained largely unused, though the turning triangle for steam locos remained, as did two short sidings adjacent to the station, used for stabling diesel locomotives.

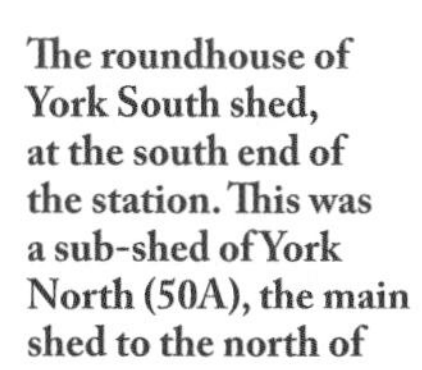

The roundhouse of York South shed, at the south end of the station. This was a sub-shed of York North (50A), the main shed to the north of

Such has been the importance of York as a railway centre that in steam's heyday, ten named expresses called at the station: 'The Aberdonian' (northbound), 'The Continental', 'The Heart of Midlothian', 'The Highlands', 'The North Briton', 'The Northumbrian', 'The Tees-Tyne Pullman' (northbound), 'The Tynesider' and 'The Scarborough Flyer'. A further seven ran through non-stop: 'The Aberdonian' (southbound), 'The Anglo-Scottish Car Carrier', 'The Elizabethan', 'The Flying Scotsman', 'The Night Scotsman', 'The Talisman' and 'The Tees-Tyne Pullman' (southbound). All these were just a part of the summer timetable that featured more than 140 weekday passenger trains departing during each 24-hour period. Thus York earned the accolade 'Gateway to the North', where rails from the South West, Midlands and across the Pennines linked into the East Coast Main Line from London to Scotland. Passengers connected between main-line expresses and local services to Leeds, Sheffield, Hull and Scarborough, while engines were changed and freight handled in the busy goods yards. A rich variety of locos could be seen on a regular basis, as examples from north, south and west mingled with the Yorkshire regulars.

As a result of Network Rail's redevelopment of the area south of York station, usually referred to as the 'Engineer's Triangle', the facility to turn steam locomotives here would have been lost had it not been for the installation of a 'new' turntable on the site next to the station avoiding line. This was originally located at Cleethorpes, but had been moved to Ferme Park, London, in the 1970s. The facility was officially declared 'open' in a formal commissioning ceremony performed by Rail Minister Simon Burns MP, when on 16 January 2013 he cut the ribbon, with ex-GWR 'Hall' No 5972 *Olton Hall* (aka *Hogwarts Castle*) providing the loading.

the station.
Above: **The new turntable is located adjacent to the Network Rail stores building in the former York Carriage Works and is accessed from the freight lines that bypass the station. The Operating Centre site is the location of the former York South engine shed, demolished in 1963; the shed's turntable pits and ground-level remains were excavated prior to the building of the new signalling centre in 2012, only to be covered over again to allow building work to continue.**

Above: **The inspection pit of one of the excavated turntables of the York South roundhouse, photographed on 27 April 2012.** ***David Vaughan Wells***

Above right: **York's ancient City Walls provide excellent vantage points from which to view its impressive historic buildings, of which the 'new' station is a fine example. To the right of the station can be seen the Royal York Hotel, an elegant Victorian building constructed as the Royal Station Hotel by the London & North Eastern Railway and set in 5 acres of landscaped gardens. It was described in *On Either Side*, a traveller's guide to features of interest to be seen from the train between London King's Cross and Edinburgh Waverley, published by the LNER in 1939, as 'one of the finest and most picturesquely placed hotels in the country, standing in magnificent grounds and affording charming views of the ancient City of York'. The guide goes on to state that 'The tariff is reasonable, the accommodation excellent and tourists desirous of breaking their journey en route between England and Scotland will be well advised to make this their stopping place.'**

In 1955 York North shed (50A) housed an allocation of 166 steam locos, including five Thompson 'A1' 4-6-2s, eight Thompson 'A2' 4-6-2s, 30 Gresley 'V2' 2-6-2s, 15 Thompson 'B1' 4-6-0s and no fewer than 46 'B16' 4-6-0s, not to mention a handful of Gresley 'D49' 4-4-0s, 'J11', 'J25' and 'J26' 0-6-0 tender locos, and several 0-6-0Ts and 0-6-0STs. To these were added ten of the powerful 'WD' 8F 2-8-0s. By 1960 York's allocation had swollen to 201 locos, with the addition of an assortment of Fowler, Stanier and Ivatt LMS designs including 2-6-4Ts, 2-6-0 Class 4s, 2-6-0 Class 2s and 0-6-0Ts, together with a couple of BR Class 3 2-6-0s. Sharing the shed space by now was the first influx of diesel locos, including nine of the new English Electric Type 4 1Co-Co1 Class, introduced in 1958, and more than 20 0-6-0 diesel shunters, also introduced during the 1950s, giving a total of 167 steam and 34 diesels shedded at 50A.

Four years later, in 1964, the diesel allocation had risen to 72 locos, while that of steam had diminished to 94. Among the remaining steam fleet, several of York's familiar classes were still represented, including the 'A1s' (whose number had by now risen to 13), the 'B1s' (now down to 11), 'B16s' (only five remaining), 'K1s' (18) and 'V2s' (26). In addition, the seven remaining 'WD' 8F 2-8-0s had been joined

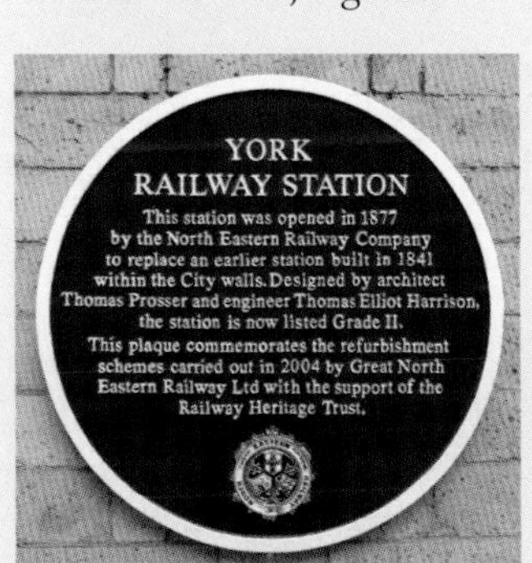

Right: **This plaque within the station celebrates the refurbishments carried out in more recent years.**

Far right: **This small plate in the paving stones forming the walkway of the City Walls opposite the station entrance points visitors in the direction of the earlier buildings.**

by eight of their big cousins, the mighty 9F 2-10-0s. Almost half of the diesel fleet consisted of English Electric 1Co-Co1s, now known as Class 40, with a sprinkling of Class 24s and a single Class 25. The remaining diesel allocation was made up of 0-6-0 diesel-mechanical and diesel-electric shunters belonging to Classes 03, 04 and 08, which by this time had replaced virtually all of York's small tank engines.

Top right: **The Worsdell Class 'D20' 4-4-0 locos, built for the NER at Gateshead from 1899 as Class 'R', were occasional visitors to York. Some examples were later modified by Gresley from 1936 and designated Class 'D20/2'. No 62375 seen here was one such 'local', being allocated to Starbeck shed near Harrogate, coded 50D, while an unmodified sister loco (classed as 'D20/1'), No 62345, was actually shedded at York in the 1950s. No 62375 was withdrawn on 31 May 1957 and cut up soon after at BR's Darlington North Road Works. York's No 62345 suffered a similar fate, and none of the class survived into preservation.**

Centre right: **A frequent visitor to the York area in the early 1960s, with classmates shedded at 50A, was Riddles War Department (Ministry of Supply) 'Austerity' 8F 2-8-0 No 90223. Introduced from 1943 and numbering more than 700 examples, these locos were purchased by British Railways in 1948. No 90223, seen here in 1961, was shedded at Leeds Neville Hill for a time, before being re-housed at Scunthorpe, Frodingham depot (36C) until her withdrawal on 31 August 1965. She was one of 42 locos cut up at Gardham, Harris & Elton's scrapyard at Chesterfield, her end coming on 31 October of that same year.**

Right: **The 'B1' Class 4-6-0s, built by the LNER and BR, numbered 410 locos, making them Thompson's most successful design, and several were deployed in the York area, being often encountered on the ECML. No 61379 *Mayflower*, seen here on 2 August 1958, was unusual in that, though she was withdrawn from service in August 1962 and cut up at BR's Doncaster Works shortly afterwards, her name lives on. Sister loco No 61306 was retired in September 1967 and preserved at Carnforth Steamtown, from where she operated 'steam specials' after her restoration to LNER livery as No 1306, carrying newly cast *Mayflower* nameplates. After periods working on the heritage Great Central Railway and Nene Valley Railway, she has more recently been overhauled again and is now back at Carnforth, in the care of West Coast Railways. No 61306 is one of only two Thompson 'B1s' to have been preserved, the other being No (6)1264 (the only LNER-built example, as 61379, though built to Thompson's LNER design, was actually a BR loco, being completed after nationalisation in 1948). No 61264 was rescued from Woodham's Barry Dock scrapyard in 1973, the only LNER loco to have been sent there. She was eventually restored and painted in BR black livery to run on the North Yorkshire Moors Railway, where she can now be seen running as sister loco No 61002 *Impala*, which was actually withdrawn and scrapped in 1967. Another name saved for posterity!**

Visiting Gresley 'A3' 'Pacific' No 60056 *Centenary* stands near the 70-foot turntable of York North shed on 11 April 1960.

The scene in the yard on 21 April 1961. The principal depot of the ex-North Eastern Railway at its headquarters and coded 50A by BR, York North catered for the main-line passenger and freight locomotives working through the area. In BR days its allocation included examples from such classes as 'A1', 'B1', 'B16', 'V2' and 'K1' from the NER and LNER, 4MTs from the LMS, ex-'WD' 2-8-0s and BR Class 9F 2-10-0s. Prominent here are 'V2' 2-6-2 No 60858, 'A1' 4-6-2 No 60129 *Guy Mannering* and 'K1' 2-6-0 No 62005. York's massive 100-foot-high reinforced concrete coaling plant, commissioned in 1932 as part of a Government-sponsored modernisation programme, had a coal capacity of 500 tons and could replenish two locos at a time, and up to 100 in a day. The 70-foot electric turntable at the north end of the yard was installed as part of the same programme. *Ben Brooksbank*

Top: **One of York North shed's 'B16/3' 4-6-0s, No 61449, is seen passing Mytholmroyd near Hebden Bridge, Calderdale, at the head of a mixed freight train on 3 August 1962. This route, opened by the Manchester & Leeds Railway in 1841 to connect these two important cities, was quickly amalgamated into the expanding Lancashire & Yorkshire Railway. The 'B16' loco design, originally introduced by Raven in 1920 as NER Class 'S3', consisted of some 70 members and featured Stephenson valve gear, but was subsequently reclassified to 'B16/1'; subsequently seven were rebuilt by Gresley from 1937 as LNER Class 'B16/2', with Walschaerts valve gear and derived motion for the inside cylinder. Later still, from 1944, 17 more were rebuilt by Thompson as Class 'B16/3' and fitted with Walschaerts valve gear for each of the three cylinders. Sixty-nine examples passed into BR ownership in 1948, the one exception being NER No 925, which was badly damaged during the Luftwaffe's 'Baedeker Air Raids' that hit York shed on the night of 28/29 April 1942. No 925 was subsequently scrapped, together with 'A4' No 4469 *Sir Ralph Wedgwood*, which was similarly destroyed at the time. Later, in 1944, 'A4' No 4466 *Herring Gull* was renamed *Sir Ralph Wedgwood* in honour of the LNER Chief Officer, a name it carried as No 60006 until it too was withdrawn in September 1965. A memorial plaque, now in the Great Hall of the National Railway Museum, marked the spot where the bomb landed, having been placed there by the Gresley Society on 29 April 1992, the 50th anniversary of the raid. No 61449 was withdrawn from service on 31 July 1963 and cut up at BR's Darlington North Road Works on 30 September. The last 'B16' was scrapped in 1964 and none survived into preservation.**

Insets: **Steamy days at York shed, with resident Peppercorn 'K1' No 62046 in the foreground. Built by the North British Locomotive Company, Glasgow, on 31 October 1949, she was withdrawn from York depot on 28 February 1967. The second picture shows another York resident, 'B16/2' No 61457, parked in store. She was a product of Darlington Works, emerging on 31 October 1923, to be withdrawn from service on 30 June 1964. Both these locos were among the 149 disposed of at Hughes Bolckow's scrapyard, North Blyth. Both photographs were taken on 11 January 1964.**

Top: **NER Class 'J72' 0-6-0T No 68712, which emerged from Darlington Works on 31 October 1920, was one of 113 built to the design by W. Worsdell and introduced from 1898. Sixteen of her classmates were allocated to York North shed at some time during their lifetime, and one, No 69023 (later named *Joem*) has been preserved, finding work on the nearby Derwent Valley Light Railway until its closure, when she was transferred to the North Yorkshire Moors Railway. No 68712 was withdrawn on 31 January 1959 and cut up at BR's Darlington North Road Works a month later on 28 February. A similar fate awaited the other 111 members of the class.**

Centre: **Raven Class 'B16/1' 4-6-0 No 61410 is seen near Cross Gates, between York and Leeds, in 1955. Built in June 1920 for the NER at Darlington Works, she was a long-term resident of York North shed, from where she was withdrawn in October 1960 and cut up that same month at BR's Darlington North Road Works.**

Right: **One of York North's clutch of 'K1' 2-6-0s, No 62065, is at work with a train of open mineral wagons in the mid-1950s.**

As the end of the steam era drew ever closer, many of the once familiar locos that graced York North depot disappeared, though a few survivors could still be seen even in 1967, and to these were added some of the lucky few that were destined for preservation.

Among the locos allocated to York shed at the nationalisation of the railways was 'A2' 'Pacific' No 60532 *Blue Peter*, destined to become the sole survivor of the class of 15 designed by Arthur Peppercorn of the LNER. Built at Doncaster Works and outshopped by the newly formed British Railways on 25 March 1948, she was later moved to Aberdeen shed to work services from there to Edinburgh, and after that was again reallocated, this time to Dundee shed. She remained in service until 1966, being the last Peppercorn 'Pacific' to be overhauled at Darlington Works. Following her withdrawal, she was put into store and was later bought by Geoff Drury, owner of 'A4' 'Pacific' *Bittern*. She was restored at York and Leeds, later being painted in LNER Apple Green as No 532 at Doncaster. Now in the care of the North Eastern Locomotive Preservation Group and housed at Barrow Hill Engine Shed in Derbyshire, she awaits funding to enable her to be restored for main-line running once more.

York North roundhouse, now the Great Hall of the National Railway Museum, closed to regular steam on Monday 12 June 1967, when its last

Left: **Stanier 'Black 5' No 44990 is seen on the turntable in York Yard during May 1967. Built at Horwich in December 1946, her final shed was 20 D Normanton, from which she was withdrawn on 31 October 1967 to become one of more than 260 locos cut up at Ward's scrapyard, Beighton, Sheffield, during steam's final years.** ***Rick Ward***

Centre and left: **This was the unhappy scene outside York North shed in February 1967, with former NER Class 'Q6' 0-8-0 No 63459 already partially dismantled. In front of her, York's own Thompson 'B1' No 61035** ***Pronghorn*** **stands equally forlorn. In the second picture, still in steam outside the shed is Peppercorn 'K1' No 62012, a visitor from Sunderland South Dock shed (54A).** ***Both Rick Ward***

Above: **Inside York North shed during February 1967, the locos assembled around the turntable include (second from left) BR Standard 5MT 4-6-0 No 73135, a visitor from Patricroft shed (26F/10C). Built at Derby Works in 1956 and fitted with Caprotti valve gear, she was withdrawn in March 1968 and cut up six months later at Cashmore's yard in Great Bridge, one of 950 locos to meet that fate.** ***Rick Ward***

five engines – four Thompson 'B1s', Nos 61030 *Nyala*, 61035 *Pronghorn*, 61319 and 61337, together with BR Standard 3MT No 77012

Below: **Further around the turntable is BR 0-6-0 Class 03 diesel-mechanical shunter No D2112 (later 03112), introduced in 1957; she is parked in the shed between empty stock movement duties in the yard. Following her withdrawal, she was bought privately and preserved, to continue working on the Boston Docks Railway, a branch from the Grantham to Skegness line in Lincolnshire, where she is still employed to take freight wagons from the shunting yard to the wharf. Sister loco No 03079 (formerly D2079) is likewise preserved privately and can now be seen working from Murton on the Derwent Valley Railway on the outskirts of York, together with former BR Class 14 0-6-0 diesel-hydraulic No D9523.** ***Rick Ward***

Above: On the opposite side of the turntable, on the extreme right, ex-LMS 'Jubilee' No 45675 *Hardy* from Leeds Holbeck shed (55A/20A) is among the locos in steam. *Rick Ward*

Left: Another view of No 45675 *Hardy* in steam at the turntable in York North shed in March 1967. Built at Crewe Works in December 1935, she was withdrawn in July 1967 and, like so many others, was scrapped that same year at Cashmore's yard at Great Bridge. *Rick Ward*

Below left: At the 'Workshops' end of York North shed, York's own Peppercorn 'K1' No 62065 is seen shortly before her withdrawal in March 1967. She was cut up at Draper's yard in Hull on 31 August of that same year, being just one of almost 600 locos to meet the same fate there. Sister loco No 62005 was more fortunate. She was the last Eastern Region locomotive in BR service when she was withdrawn from Leeds Holbeck shed on 30 December 1967, and survived into preservation, though originally only as a source of a spare boiler for the solitary preserved 'K4'. Later, in 1972, she was donated to the North Eastern Locomotive Preservation Group as the sole surviving class member, and by 1975 had been returned to full main-line running order. Now named *Lord of the Isles* and based on the North Yorkshire Moors Railway, No 62005 has enjoyed several memorable seasons on the summer Fort William to Mallaig 'Jacobite' service, recalling fond memories of the 'K1s' in Scotland. *Rick Ward*

A pair of survivors are seen together in the shed, also during February 1967. LNER 'A4' No 4498 *Sir Nigel Gresley* stands alongside sister loco No 60019 *Bittern*. *Rick Ward*

– were transferred away, replaced by brand-new Class 20 and Class 47 diesels, which left preserved 'A4' No 60019 *Bittern* as the only serviceable steam locomotive on the premises.

Happily, this was not the end of steam in York – far from it. The city that inspired George Hudson to remark that his intention was to 'mak all t'railways cum t'York' drew steam specials from far and wide, as it still does to this day.

The long and curved platforms of York station made it necessary to provide electric bells in order to facilitate the starting of trains, the use of which was

Another loco destined for preservation found a temporary home in York shed towards the end of the steam era. Peppercorn 'A2' 'Pacific' No 60532 *Blue Peter* is seen (right) awaiting restoration following her withdrawal in 1966, stabled alongside No 60019 *Bittern*. *Rick Ward*

Posing in the yard shortly after her restoration in the workshops at York, Leeds and Doncaster, *Blue Peter* is resplendent in Apple Green livery and carrying what would have been her LNER number, 532. *Rick Ward*

Above: **GWR 'Castle' No 7029 *Clun Castle* is coaled in York Yard after bringing in the Ian Allan 'Silver Jubilee' tour from London King's Cross on 8 October 1967. *Rick Ward***

Above right: **At York station at the head of the Railway Correspondence & Travel Society (West Riding Branch) 'A4 to Edinburgh' tour is preserved 'A4' No 60019 *Bittern*. Steam-hauled from Leeds City via York to Edinburgh Waverley and return, 'No 19' handled the charter faultlessly on 4 November 1967. *Rick Ward***

Centre right: **Being coaled from the back of a lorry in York Yard after hauling 'The Yorkshire Harvester' tour is LNER Gresley 'A3' No 4472 *Flying Scotsman*. The train, from King's Cross to York on 6 October 1968, was run as a fund-raising venture for York Minster in connection with its Harvest Festival service. *Rick Ward***

Right: **Another famous Gresley engine, 'A4' No 4498, named after its designer, and a popular visitor following the official 'end of steam', is seen here in York Yard in about 1970. *Rick Ward***

Far left and Left: **There was to be no happy ending for these two locos as the cutter's torch gets to work on 8F No 48763 and former Lostock Hall 'Black 5' No 44942 in 1967.** ***Both Rick Ward***

Below: **The end is nigh, and not only for the locos. These reminders of the Steam Age in York Yard would also soon be swept away in the name of progress.** ***Rick Ward***

Below: **York's impressive mechanical coaling plant, seen here in 1967, was erected in 1932 in the shed yard. It survived until 1970 and was only brought down with considerable difficulty.**

On 22 March 1970 explosive charges attached to the legs were detonated, but failed to bring down the plant, which was left leaning precariously. Later, attempts to pull it down by means of cables attached to four diesel locomotives also failed to budge it, the cables repeatedly snapping under the strain.

Finally, in May of that year it was eventually levelled by means of a heavy metal ball swung repeatedly at it by a crane. ***Author/Rick Ward (2)***

governed by an addition to the Rule Book: 'Guards-in-charge of trains must use these bells to indicate to the front Guard that the train is ready to start, and the latter, on hearing the bell, may signal the train away in the usual manner. When there is only one Guard with a train, drivers may accept the ringing of a bell as a signal to start, instead of a green flag or light referred to in Rule 141.'

The railway workshops at York date from those of the Y&NMR of 1839, and though the emphasis was always on the repair and

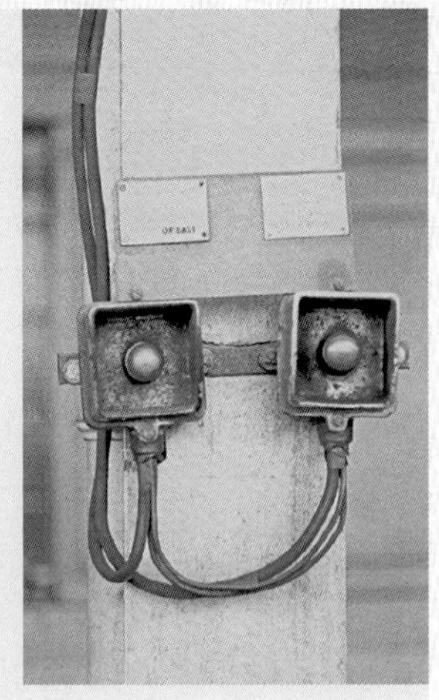

Above: **The bells for use by train Guards at Platform 14, photographed on 7 September 1975. The plate above the left bell-push reads '14 Platform Drivers Starting Bell, North or East', while that above the right bell-push reads '14 Plat. Train Ready to Start North Bound'.**

Above: **In a quiet corner on what is now Platform 9, paraffin lamps are left to be collected by Guards, with the chalked instruction on the blackboard: 'Will guards sign for tail lamps in book provided'. 21 September 1975.**

upgrading of locos rather than the construction of new ones, the works at Queen Street became extensive, comprising Boiler Shop, Machine Shop and Paint Shop, in addition to a range of other general maintenance facilities. It also became important for the construction and repair of carriages and wagons, though by 1865 the facility was considered outdated and the NER began building new premises nearby to concentrate on the building of wagons and carriages. A change of policy by the NER in 1900 led to the transfer of all engine building and repairs to Darlington, followed by the closure of York Engine Works in 1905. The now redundant 'Shops' were converted into an engine shed for locos from visiting railway companies, though this work was also later transferred to York North shed and the buildings later become the main display area of the original York Railway Museum and home to some of the facilities provided for NER staff as part of the company's Railway Institute.

The NER's 'new' wagon and carriage works in York were opened in 1865, growing rapidly from its conception to occupy some 17 acres near North Junction, building and repairing a variety of freight rolling stock until its closure by BR in 1965 following a severe decline in the railway freight business. The site was never abandoned, however, and some wagon repairing and other work continued under the auspices of Freightliner Group Limited, which now operates the facility.

The carriage works, opposite on the south side of the line near North Junction, constructed originally from the early 1880s, also grew rapidly to engulf more than 45 acres, employing a workforce in the region of 5,500 at its height. It quickly established a reputation as an important site for the development and construction of a wide variety of rolling stock. In the years following the Second World War production consisted mainly of standard carriages and vestibule brake-vans, but by the late 1950s this had been extended to include Buffet Open 2nd and Sleeper 1st stock. In 1958 the first electric multiple units (EMUs) with overhead pick-ups were built for the London, Tilbury & Southend (LT&S) route. Such work would dominate production throughout the 1960s and '70s, with stock being outshopped in quantity for the Liverpool Street, Clacton and Walton line and for Brighton and Bournemouth trains, as well as for the LT&S. Also, by this time loco-hauled Travelling Post Office vehicles were being constructed, as were the prototype steel framework and aluminium panelling sets.

A cast-iron carriage plate from York-built 2nd Open Tourist Mark II Type 3202 coach in the number series 5070-5202.

A plate from one of the last batch of Travelling Post Office (TPO) Sorting Vans to come out of the York Works, in the number series 80362-80374. TPOs were a network of mail trains that sorted the mail while en route. The service ceased on 9 January 2004, though several vehicles are preserved, such as the last one in the above series, No 80374, on the heritage Battlefield Line in Leicestershire.

Throughout the 1970s, production of Class 312, 313 and 314 electric units for the Waterloo to Bournemouth route continued, supplemented by vehicles for the Great Northern Outer programme, Birmingham-Coventry, Liverpool-Southport-Ormskirk and the Clyde Rail routes. Some overseas orders were also fulfilled at this time, including nine diesel power cars for Northern Ireland and 13 five-car EMUs for Taiwan. By the 1980s Class 508 stock for the Southern Region dominated production, together with Class 315 for Sleaford and Class 317 vehicles for Moorgate-Bedford trains. During the latter half of the 1980s output turned to the production of Class 150 'Sprinter' diesel multiple units (DMUs), in addition to Class 319 and 321 electric stock for Thameslink. This was a very busy time at the carriage works, and 1989 saw the construction of ten two-car third-rail electric units for the Docklands Light Railway, followed in 1991 by three Class 321 four-car sets for the West Yorkshire Passenger Transport Executive, supplementing orders for its Class 319 DMU and Class 465 EMU sets. That year also saw work start on the all-aluminium-bodied Class 165 vehicles and on a consignment of 25 articulated units for Eurotram, Strasbourg.

Output of two- and three-car DMUs and four-car third-rail pick-up and dual-voltage EMUs continued until the end of production in 1995.

The former British Rail Engineering Limited (BREL) York carriage works finally closed in 1996 while in the ownership of Asea Brown Boveri (ABB), one of the world's largest engineering and conglomerate companies with headquarters in Zurich, Switzerland, after a period during which the workforce had been progressively reduced in response to a gradual decline in orders for new stock. Part of the former carriage works site was then reopened by Thrall Europa from 1997, continuing the long association with railway wagon manufacturing in the area by assembling wagons supplied in 'kit form' for the freight operating company English, Welsh & Scottish Railway (EWS). Sadly, this reprieve was to

Left: **The extensive York South Yards extend towards Skelton Junction, a mile away to the north, as LNER 'B1' 4-6-0 No 61353 threads its train along the York avoiding lines on 25 June 1964. On the right is York Wagon Works, while to the left beyond the diesel shunter lie the vast Carriage Works.** ***Ben Brooksbank***

The former York Wagon Works is now operated by Freightliner, as seen on 4 July 2013. The former York Carriage Works is opposite to the left, across the tracks, with the new turntable beyond that.

last only until 2002. The site is now known as National Rail, Holgate Road, and is used to undertake maintenance of engineering rolling stock and as an active base for infrastructure operations, in particular 'rail-head treatment trains' (RHTT), operated by Direct Rail Services.

Last 'Pacific' to York

The final BR steam-hauled working into York by a 'Pacific' Class loco is believed to have been the Fridays-only Manchester to York service, usually a 'Black 5' rostering, the last of which arrived at the station at about 20.30 on 28 December 1967 hauled by BR 'Britannia' Class 7P6F No 70013 *Oliver Cromwell*. Built at Crewe and introduced into traffic on 30 May 1951, she re-entered that works again on 3 October 1966 to become the last BR steam locomotive to undergo a routine heavy overhaul, being outshopped on 2 February 1967 following a special ceremony to mark the end of 123 years of building and repairing steam locos on the site. Works Manager John Barker-Wyatt commented: 'The age of steam, although nostalgic, is over and we welcome the new era of diesel.'

In the summer of 1968, No 70013 was chosen as one of four steam locomotives to haul the now legendary 'Fifteen Guinea Special' from Liverpool via Manchester to Carlisle and back (the other three locos being 'Black 5' Nos 45110, 44781 and 44871). The trip, train 1T57, on 11 August 1968, was hailed as the last main-line passenger train to be hauled by a steam locomotive on BR prior to the 'steam ban' that would start the following day. The occasion was not without its problems, however. A thousand steam fans arrived at Manchester's Victoria station expecting to pay the usual price of threepence for a platform ticket, only to be informed that the charge on this occasion would be 10 times that, at 2s 6d. To add insult to injury, when these special 'souvenir' tickets ran out, enthusiasts were still charged the full price but only received the normal threepenny version of the ticket. The inflated price of the train tickets (£15 15s in pre-decimal currency, estimated to be more than £400 today) also came in for heavy criticism, with British Rail being accused of profiteering at the expense of the enthusiasts. The high price was explained as being due to the great demand to travel on what was believed to be the last ever steam-hauled main-line passenger train and the extra costs involved in staging this 'unique' event.

No 70013 was preserved and became a part of the National Collection immediately following the 'Fifteen Guinea Special'. In 2008 she was temporarily renumbered as 70048 and renamed *The Territorial Army 1908-2008* to celebrate the 100th anniversary of the TA. In steam days, sister 'Britannia' Class loco No 70048 was named *The Territorial Army 1908-1958*; she was built in July 1954, withdrawn on 6 May 1967 and cut up at McWilliams's scrapyard, Shettleston, Glasgow, on 12 September of that year, one of more than 200 steam locos to be so dealt with in that yard, including 21 other 'Britannias' out of the original total of 55. Other than No 70013, only No 70000, *Britannia* herself, survives.

In subsequent years No 70013 became a frequent choice of traction for the 'Scarborough Spa Express', centred on York, as well as gracing the tracks at the head of numerous other tours and charters. On 11 August 2013, to mark the 45th anniversary of 1T57, she was involved in a second 're-run' of the famous train

Top: **A 'standard issue' 3d platform ticket from Manchester Victoria station, which was being sold at 10 times its usual price to enthusiasts wanting to see the 'Fifteen Guinea Special' leave on 11 August 1968.**

Above: **'Britannia' Class No 70013 *Oliver Cromwell* heads 1T57, the 'Fifteen Guinea Special' on 11 August 1968, about to depart from Manchester Victoria for Carlisle.**

Right: **'Double-headed' with Stanier 8F No 48151, *Oliver Cromwell*, running as No 70048, is seen passing Colton Junction, York, with the returning 'Help 4 Heroes' Lancaster-York special on 27 March 2010.**

(the first having been the 40th anniversary re-run in 2008), accompanied by 'Black 5' Nos 45305, 44871 and 44932 running as 44781, the only one of the original three participants from that class not to be subsequently preserved. No 45305 had been allocated to the 1968 1T57 train, but had failed the night before, to be replaced by No 45110, so it is fitting that she got a chance to appear at last on the re-run.

Restored to her more familiar number and name, No 70013 *Oliver Cromwell* storms away from York through Towthorpe on 30 August 2011 in charge of the 'Scarborough Spa Express'.

2. After the Age of Steam

The end of the Steam Age on our railways signalled far more than the loss of locomotives, ushering in as it did a new era of railway modernisation. In the years that followed 1968, there came about a restructuring of the system that had at its core the principle that Britain's network needed to be radically overhauled, to be transformed into a more efficient, more advanced and more attractive operation, which in turn would lead to more

investment and ultimately generate more income from both the passenger and freight sectors.

The first and most noticeable change was of course the traction. Steam was finished and, not only that, any prospect that the fledgling preservation movement might somehow save cherished locomotives and run them on the national network was dealt an immediate blow by the 'steam ban' that was immediately put into place. At the same time, there came into being a policy that 'old is bad, new is good'. A consequence of that philosophy was the fairly rapid removal of once familiar items from the Steam Age. In the cause of modernisation, many of our long-cherished railway fixtures and fittings have been 'rationalised' or have simply disappeared, almost overnight.

The signal box is a case in point. York station and its radiating lines were controlled by a host of boxes, some in and around the station and its yards and others along the various diverging lines. They ranged in size from the small – little more than cabins with a handful of levers to control a crossing – to very substantial – containing more than 100 levers. In 1937 one of the largest contracts ever awarded to a railway signalling contractor was given to the Westinghouse Brake & Signal Company for the installation of a system of colour-light signals extending from Copmanthorpe and Naburn, on the Leeds and London lines respectively, about 4 miles south of York, to Poppleton Junction, about 1½ miles to the north, there to join up with the existing colour-light system to Thirsk and Northallerton. This involved the provision of a new signal box in the centre of York station.

Work on the scheme was interrupted by the Second World War, but the new 'power box' was finally opened for business in May 1951, when it became one of the largest route-relay interlockings in the world. Its opening made several of York's large and hitherto important boxes redundant, including the largest, Locomotive Yard, which at the time was the largest mechanical signal box in the UK. All told, the York power box replaced seven mechanical boxes containing a total of 868 levers, the most notable of which were Waterworks Box, at the north end of the station (132 levers), Clifton Junction (120 levers), Leeman Road (91 levers), and Platform, at the centre of the station, controlling the crossovers (80 levers). The power box itself was unobtrusive, being located above the buildings that separate the platforms then numbered 13 and 14 (now Platforms 8 and 9), just to the north of the footbridge. Having no direct sight of the trains, the signalmen within would control the progress of their trains by means of track circuit lights on their display panels.

The location of the power box at York station is betrayed by the bay window and doorway to its left, above Platform 8. Its relay room, 46 metres long and 10 metres wide, contained nearly 3,000 relays, and the box controlled more than 33 miles of track and replaced seven manual signal boxes. A corresponding window above Platform 9, seen in the second picture, identifies the opposite side of the room, below which East Coast Railways power car No 91125 pauses with a train from King's Cross to Edinburgh on 31 January 2013.

Above: **The former Platform signal box survives above the bookshop at the station entrance, and is now a popular cafe, with access from steps on the footbridge.**

The observant visitor to York station can still find reminders of steam days long gone, like these signal wire pulleys amongst the girders at the end of the footbridge outside what was Platform signal box.

In its turn, the 1951 power box was itself replaced when in 1989 York's Integrated Electronic Control Centre was opened, sounding the death knell first for other local boxes, then, as its influence was extended, the power boxes at Tollerton, Thirsk and Northallerton, followed in the early 2000s by Leeds. Now the overall control area is from Temple Hirst near Doncaster in the south to Danby Wiske near Northallerton in the north, and from Gargrave near Skipton in the west through Leeds to York via Church Fenton, totalling more than 200 miles of track.

Another York box that disappeared at about this time was Burton Lane, situated on the Scarborough line about a mile from York station and originally controlling a crossing, which was soon replaced by a bridge, the Foss Islands branch with its access to the Rowntrees chocolate factory private station for the workforce, Foss Islands goods depot, the local gas and electricity works and the Derwent Valley Light Railway (DVLR), all sadly no longer with us. The 32-lever box was opened in 1878 and closed on 30 April 1989.

The Selby to Driffield line was closed by BR in 1964 as part of the 'Beeching cuts',

Above: **One of the surviving freight services from the Foss Islands branch joins the Scarborough to York line at Burton Lane on 24 August 1981, with a Class 08 shunter in charge. Note the NER lower-quadrant semaphore signal. Taken on the same day, the second picture shows a DMU waiting to collect workers from Rowntrees Factory Halt.**

thus isolating the DVLR; successive sections were then closed due to lack of traffic, until by 1973 only about 4 miles from Layerthorpe to Dunnington remained operative. With the closure of the company's last major source of freight, Yorkshire Grain Driers Ltd at special passenger trains. York's local newspaper, the *Yorkshire Evening Press*, heralded the venture on 9 September 1976 with the headline 'Steam train trips from York planned' and went on to describe how the trains would use rolling stock from the NRM hauled initially

Dunnington, the line was doomed, in spite of an attempt by the owners of the independent freight-only line to join forces with the newly opened National Railway Museum in a last-ditch attempt to revive its fortunes by using NER Class 'J72' 0-6-0T *Joem* and ex LNWR 'Precedent' Class No 790 *Hardwicke* to haul

Above: **Improvements to York's road transport system also had their effect on the city's railway. In the early 1960s a new bridge was built over the lines at York Yard North, necessitating alterations to the signal box over which the road to Clifton would pass, including the loss of its traditional-style roof. Originally named Severus Junction, the box did not operate the main-line signals, only those on the goods lines between Holgate Junction and Skelton Junction. York Yard North box, as it became known, is seen here on 10 February 1980; it had 150 levers, though this was later reduced to just 60, before it became one of the casualties of the resignalling of 1989.**

Right: **The 'steam train trips' day on Saturday 9 October 1976 featured ex-LNWR No 790 *Hardwicke* hauling several trains between York's Layerthorpe station and Dunnington, a distance of about 4 miles – and certainly attracted an appreciative audience.**

Bootham signal box controlled a crossing half a mile further along the same line, where it crossed the road to Helmsley near the Rowntrees factory, which can be seen in the background. This was the junction of the line to Market Weighton, Beverley and Hull by way of Stamford Bridge and Pocklington, also long gone. It is seen here on 25 April 1976, but in 1989 it too was to suffer the same fate as Burton Lane box.

On the East Coast Main Line, 5½ miles north of York, was located the tiny station serving Shipton by Beningbrough, an early casualty of the relentless march of progress. Complete with sidings for goods traffic controlled by its own signal box and a platform for local stopping trains, it closed to passengers on 15 September 1958, and to goods traffic from 5 May 1965.

by *Hardwicke* and possibly connecting with the NRM by means of a vintage bus such as an open-topped charabanc. Following a successful test run a week later, a day of steam train trips was organised for 9 October, when three runs were made in each direction to test the viability of a summer tourist service the following year. The result was described as 'very encouraging' in the *Evening Press* of 11 October, with 300 passengers having been carried.

The East Coast Main Line south from York branched from the York to Leeds line at

Right: **Further north towards Thirsk was the tiny box at Pilmoor, seen here as Class 37 No 37163 heads north with a mixed freight on 11 April 1975.**

Centre: **'Deltic' No 55009 *Alycidon* races off the ECML at Challoner's Whin Junction to join the Leeds line for the final sprint into York, making light work of the 12.00 departure from London King's Cross, the Sunday 'Aberdonian', on 6 June 1976.**

Bottom: **On the line from Leeds once stood the station serving the charming village of Bolton Percy. Opened in 1839, it was modified in 1904 when the line was widened to four tracks, at which time the new signal box seen here in March 1975 was added. Sadly this station and the signal box that accompanied it have long gone, as have the signs and notices that were so often associated with railway property.**

Challoner's Whin Junction in Dringhouses, and continued through Selby to Doncaster. However, concerns relating to anticipated mining subsidence in the Selby Coalfield, together with bottleneck problems at Selby station, resulted in the Selby Diversion being constructed and opened in 1983. The new route continued south past Challoner's Whin towards Leeds, then at Colton, 8 miles from York, a new junction took it directly to just north of Doncaster, there to rejoin the 'old' ECML at Temple Hirst Junction.

The prospects for the surviving signal boxes remains worrying, however, as indications are that they may soon become a thing of the past…

Above: **On the gate to the station at Bolton Percy on the same day, the instruction is clear. Sadly the site is now levelled and the signal box is no more, though the land has been reclaimed by the Yorkshire Wildlife Trust and developed as a Nature Reserve.**

Left and above: **Marston Moor is a quiet country station on the Harrogate to York line, now reduced to single track. Seen here in March 1975, it still had a working platform, a crossing box and a keeper to manually operate the heavy crossing gates and semaphore signals.**

Right: **Marston Moor crossing box was still operative in April 2013, though now the station is closed and the platforms overgrown. The heavy wooden gates have been replaced by lightweight tubular steel ones fitted with rubber-tyred wheels, and the cast-iron North Eastern Railway 'Warning to Trespassers' sign is also long gone. The semaphore signals survive, however, but, like so much else along such branch lines, their days are numbered with the construction of York's new Rail Operating Centre, estimated to take over control in the next four to five years.**

Above: and above right **Happily, not all signal boxes in the York region have been swept away in the name of progress. The line to Scarborough, through the market town of Malton, has so far retained a number of classics, including that in the picturesque valley of the River Derwent at Kirkham Abbey, which controls the level crossing on the approach to the river and the ruins of the nearby monastery, the gates still being operated by means of a wheel in the box. Nearer York, in the village of Strensall, the second picture shows that the crossing box was still going strong on 1 July 2011, though here the manually operated gates have been upgraded to electrically operated barriers, equipped with warning lights.**

Above: **Starbeck station, in the eastern suburbs of Harrogate, dates from September 1848. Though now reduced to an unmanned halt and passing place on the sadly 'singled' line between York and Harrogate and on to Leeds, trains once called here en route to Pateley Bridge, Pannal, Ripon and Northallerton. The then junction boasted an important engine shed (coded 50D), goods shed and extensive sidings, all controlled by two signal boxes, of which only Starbeck South (now simply Starbeck) remains in business.**

Left: **One reminder of the Steam Age that has survived at York is this North Eastern Railway water tower, tucked away behind the buildings at the south end of the station close to the site of the former Queen Street Locomotive Works, in an area now used as a car park.**

3. Railway infrastructure – heritage or burden?

From the end of steam through to the 1990s, our railways underwent a massive yet much-needed transformation, both in terms of traction and infrastructure. Haulage had changed dramatically since the arrival of the DMU, EMU and HST sets, with a corresponding decline in the prevalence of locomotive-hauled trains and with them the number of maintenance depots and main-line workshops needed to service them. At the same time we have seen the demise of countless signal boxes and traditional level crossings, with their crossing-keepers and heavy wooden gates, to be replaced by automatic barriers operated by the approaching trains. Similarly, many stations are now unstaffed and the trains controlled from a small number of highly sophisticated main control centres.

All of these changes have contributed to the desired effect of reducing costs and improving efficiency, so much so that in recent years our railways have experienced a great increase in use. However, the situation regarding signal boxes deserves further attention, as an article in the December 2011 issue of *Railtalk* magazine pointed out, reporting that in July 2011 Network Rail announced its operating strategy to cover the next 30 years of signalling with a plan to modernise the system by consolidating the activities of hundreds of signal boxes nationwide into just 14 'Rail Operating Centres', six of which are existing Operating Centres – at Ashford, Cardiff, Derby, Edinburgh, Gillingham and Saltley. Two further existing Operating Centres, at Didcot and Glasgow, will be upgraded, with six new buildings being constructed at Basingstoke, Manchester, Romford, Rugby, Three Bridges and York. The plan would mean that more than 800 signal boxes currently in operation would become redundant, including around 40 in England alone that currently have 'Listed Building' status.

Organisations concerned about the loss of such historically important parts of our railway infrastructure are working to devise a strategy that will see the most significant signal boxes preserved and safeguarded for future generations. To this end, the National Railway Museum, English Heritage, Historic Scotland and the Railway Heritage Trust are working closely with Network Rail on a comprehensive review of all signal boxes with the aim of saving those of particular historical or social significance.

As a result of the concerns outlined above,

Construction work for the York Rail Operating Centre goes ahead on a very wet site during March 2013, its skeleton already covering the remains of the former roundhouse. The station avoiding lines are on the right and the lifted section of the former 'Engineer's Triangle' on the left. This will be the largest of the network of 14 Rail Operating Centres that will control virtually the country's entire railway system. In addition there will also be a Workforce Development Centre to cater for training needs and office facilities for staff from the various train operating companies. Network Rail plans to consolidate all signalling and control activity into its Rail Operating Centres over the next 15-30 years.

and responding to the resignalling plans made public by Network Rail in the autumn of 2011, research was carried out between October 2011 and February 2012 by English Heritage that aimed to provide a national overview of signal boxes, both operational Network Rail boxes and those out of use, on heritage railways and in museums. The results, published as Research Report Series No 28-2012, 'Railway Signal Boxes – a Review', under the authorship of John Minnis, notes that 80% of Network Rail's traditional signal boxes are expected to disappear within the next 15 years, and seeks to identify the most significant remaining examples and make recommendations as to those that should go forward for assessment for 'Listing'. It aims to fill in gaps in existing listings to ensure that a representative sample of the principal types is protected.

In Appendix 1 of the Review, 86 Network Rail traditional signal boxes are identified as being currently Listed, as well as a further three swing bridge boxes. Appendix 2 lists 68 boxes selected for assessment for possible Listing based on the Review, of which 49 are Network Rail boxes, with the remainder already on heritage railways. It is worth remembering, as the Review points out, that the number of traditional mechanical signal boxes has been reduced steadily from around 10,000 at nationalisation in 1948 to fewer than 500 on the network today, with line closures and the introduction of new signalling technology contributing to the decline. If the recommendations of the Review were to be accepted and the boxes selected for assessment and subsequently 'Listed', we would be left with fewer than 160 traditional signal boxes in the country, including those already 'saved' on heritage lines. This must surely be a 'wake-up call' to enthusiasts everywhere, to take up cameras and record the survivors before they disappear in the name of progress.

For those interested in this aspect of our railway heritage, John Hinson's *Directory of British Signal Boxes* lists what he describes as 'all signal boxes known to have ever existed', but he does add that though this is the aim, the listing can never claim to be complete as new information is continually being discovered. Nevertheless, by my estimation, his Directory lists somewhere in the region of 18,000 signal boxes!

The signal boxes represent perhaps one of the more noticeable memories of the Steam Age that is being swept away, but with them have also gone many of the artefacts that served as poignant reminders of our railway history. Much of this once-familiar lineside 'furniture' – cast-iron signs dating from the pre-Grouping era, for instance – has disappeared in recent years, and although examples can

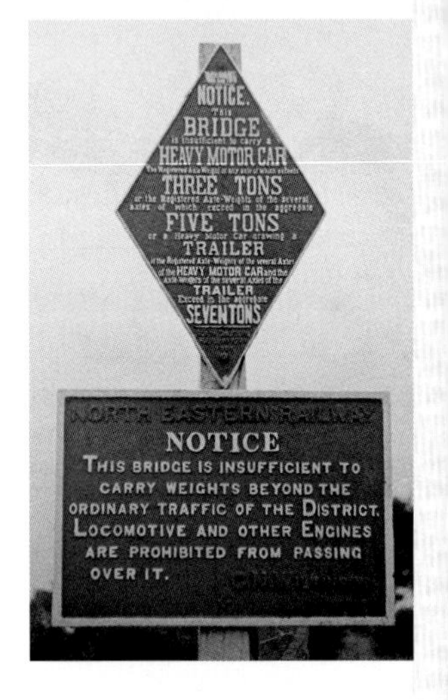

Once a common sight at crossings and bridges throughout the network, signs like these advised of local restrictions or warned would-be trespassers of the possible consequences, which very often involved a fine of 'Forty Shillings' (£2). The North Eastern Railway 'trespass notice' stood by a public foot-crossing next to the site of the former ECML station at Beningbrough, just north of York, and was photographed during May 1975. The other picture shows a pair of NER bridge 'weight restriction' signs that adorned the bridge beyond the station, recorded in July 1975.

Right and far right: **This now rare example of an NER 'diamond' bridge weight restriction sign and one of the once abundant NER 'trespass notices' are now fully restored and preserved on the North Yorkshire Moors Railway.**

Below right: **Just north of York near the village of Shipton by Beningbrough, this large lineside sign, photographed on 18 May 1978, indicates the distance still to be travelled by trains on the East Coast Main Line to the Scottish capital.**

Far right: **A short distance further north, near the village of Tollerton, one of the more unusual lineside signs is this 'Half Way' sign photographed in August 1976.**

still be viewed at the National Railway Museum in York and in the collections of the heritage railways, finding one still in its original setting is rare indeed.

Main-line signals in the York area have been of the 'colour-light' variety for more than half a century, though along the branch lines semaphore posts survive as they do elsewhere on the network, though the NER 'slotted' lower-quadrant type was both unusual and rare. Fortunately, at least one example survives to be admired by those with the time and inclination to appreciate it.

Finally, among those railway features that we have known and loved for so long, but which today are also under threat,

One of the few examples of an NER 'slotted' lower-quadrant semaphore signal to be found in the York area is this one, which adorned the Derwent Valley Light Railway line just beyond its station at Layerthorpe, photographed on 7 August 1980. A second was located on the Scarborough line near Haxby, and this one survives, preserved within the entrance area at York station, seen here on 27 January 1984, shortly after its restoration and erection.

are level crossings. Network Rail has closed 600 level crossings since 2009, with around 100 having gone in the last year and a further 150 earmarked to disappear over the next 18 months. The majority of the closures involve those crossings operated by users, most of which are in rural areas. In addition, about 150 footpath crossings have also been closed, out of a total of about 2,500 user-worked crossings, 3,000 footpath crossings and about 200 station crossings.

The reason given for this policy is quite simply to improve user safety. Among the measures being implemented by Network Rail as part of its £130 million investment programme to improve level crossing safety are:

- Replacing footpath crossings with footbridges
- Installing warning lights at footpath crossings
- A schools education programme called 'Rail Safe' to explain level crossing safety
- Increased use of technology such as camera enforcement vans, better barrier control systems, and obstacle detection lasers.

Source: *Railtalk* magazine, Issue 74, November 2012

According to data released by the Rail Safety & Standards Board, published by *The Guardian* on 10 May 2010, 13 people had died and 145 motorists (about three per week) had narrowly avoided fatal collisions with a train in the previous year at level crossings in Great Britain. There were more than 3,000 recorded incidents of motorist or pedestrian misuse or error in that period, constituting, according to Network Rail, 95% of all level crossing incidents. That said, in recent years Great Britain's level crossings have proved among the safest in Europe, both in terms of actual fatalities and fatal incidents per 100,000 of the population.

During 2013, in response to increasing concerns about the use of level crossings, Network Rail announced its intension to improve user safety at three on the York to Harrogate line. Work will be carried out at stations at Poppleton, Cattal and Hammerton to prevent pedestrians, cyclists and passengers crossing the tracks in an unsafe manner.

This typical farm crossing operated by the user on a rural line is near Haxby, just outside York, on the line to Scarborough. It is equipped with instructions for safe use and a telephone in case of problems.

In an altogether more testing location, this foot crossing at Railway Cottages, near Shipton by Beningbrough, requires users – including families living in the row of houses beyond the gates – to negotiate the four-track 'racing stretch' of the East Coast Main Line north of York. The sign to the right reads 'High Speed Trains in excess of 100mph pass this point. Take extra care when crossing the line.' Good advice! These two photographs were taken on 27 November 2012.

4. Maintaining the permanent way

A love of trains is not just about the past. For any railway system to function safely and effectively, the infrastructure needs to be cared for, monitored and improved. Inspecting and maintaining the 'permanent way' – the railway lines that carry the trains as opposed to the 'temporary way' often laid by contractors (particularly in the early days) to transport material and spoil about the site, which would be taken up when the permanent track was completed – is and always has been of the utmost importance for the safe running of trains.

Above: **An example of a derelict LNER concrete platelayers' hut beside the Leeds-York line near Bolton Percy, as seen on 3 October 2012.**

Above right: **A lengthman in his 'high-vis' suit walks a length of the line between Leeds and York near Bolton Percy on 3 October 2012, and acknowledges the 'whistle' from the driver of First Trans-Pennine's Middlesbrough to Manchester Airport Class 185 'Desiro' set No 185110.**

An early form of railway was the initially horse-drawn 'plateway', widely adopted in Britain, which consisted of short cast-iron flanged plates resting on stone blocks, sometimes without sleepers. These 3-foot lengths would often spread apart, increasing the gauge and causing chaos and derailments, so were in time replaced by the more modern rolled wrought-iron (later steel) 'edge-rails' used to this day, where the flange is on the vehicle wheels rather than on the track. Men called 'platelayers' were responsible for laying and maintaining these tracks, and the name has survived into modern railway usage. A platelayer would typically be responsible for inspecting and maintaining his length of track, including the sleepers and the 'fishplates' joining the lengths of rail, and would also grease the points and watch out for any wear and tear on the actual rails. His shelter or base would be the platelayers' hut, from which he would patrol his section daily, walking perhaps up to 10 miles. Large numbers of these huts can still be seen at the lineside today, though they are often now in an abandoned and dilapidated condition.

Platelayers, or 'lengthmen' as they could also be known, might work in gangs on busy lines, perhaps with a 'look-out' to warn of approaching trains, which could be difficult to hear (especially diesels or the even quieter electrics), even though the driver would sound a warning. If the wind was blowing in the wrong direction, it could become a frighteningly close thing.

Visual inspection of the track still occurs and is an important aspect of railway safety, but as trains pass over the rails they gradually cause their deformation due to flexing of the rail, compression of the ballast and the creation of voids under the sleepers. This can cause tilting of the track and increase the risk of a derailment. The traditional way of measuring track deflection is by use of the 'Voidmeter'.

Useful though Voidmeters were, they could only provide a limited amount of data, and increasingly more sophisticated methods are being employed to inspect and monitor the railway system. Network Rail operates a range of high-tech Track Maintenance Vehicles (TMVs), which have increasingly replaced the army of platelayers and lengthmen on whose diligence we have depended for so long.

Above: **This instrument, the Abtus Voidmeter, measures the deflection of the track as a train passes over it, determining the efficiency of the ballast. The graduations on the scale represent units of ballast necessary to cure the deflection. In more modern versions, the amount of movement is converted to an electronic signal, which is then monitored by a central computer.**

Left: **Hand-operated track-monitoring equipment like this seen in use at Holgate Junction near York on 4 June 2013, gives detailed information about the condition of the track, which is instantly analysed by the on-board computer to diagnose any potential problem. Such equipment, being easily transportable, gives the track maintenance crews vital up-to-date data on which to act.**

Matissa R24S Ballast Regulator Vehicle No DR 77801, operated by Volker-Rail, passes Colton Junction near York on 17 August 2012.

Right: **There is still a place for the traditional ways of working, as a Colas Rail permanent way gang shovel ballast on the East Coast Main Line near Shipton by Beningbrough, north of York, on 5 October 2012.**

Below and below right: **At the south end of York station on 16 April 2013, a Network Rail track gang work to level the tracks, while nearby their look-out blows his warning horn to indicate the approach of a train.**

Left: **A look-out waves his 'Advance Look-Out' blue and white chequered warning flag and sounds his horn, protecting a permanent way gang working at Colton Junction on the approach to York, where a long bend taken at speed could jeopardise those working on the track. The warning would be repeated by another look-out closer to the gang.**

On a modern high-speed, high-density railway network it has become increasingly important to establish and maintain the highest standards of safety and reliability, and consequently the array of machines developed by specialist manufacturers to achieve this is impressive. Perhaps the most often seen TMVs are the 'tamping machines' or 'ballast tampers', used to push the ballast under the track, a very important and continuously necessary task that is increasingly rarely carried out manually due to the now extensive use of heavy concrete sleepers. Such machines are manufactured by specialist infrastructure service providers such as Volker-Rail, based at Doncaster, part of the Netherlands-based Volker-Wessels civil engineering and construction group. As well as ballast tampers, the company supplies cranes and other rail maintenance equipment, fulfilling a large part of the network tamping contract for Network Rail. Swietelsky-Babcock Rail (SB Rail) is also an important track renewal company operating on-track plant such as tamping machines, inspection vehicles and heavy-duty cranes for Network Rail. This is perhaps the UK's leading engineering support service organisation, heavily involved in defence, energy and telecommunications, as well as transport.

Network Rail operates a range of 'on-track plant' that has largely replaced the railway gangs aided by steam cranes and mechanical

Above: **Volker Rail Matissa B45 Tamper TMV No DR 75303 runs past the site of the former station at Bolton Percy, between Leeds and York, on 19 September 2012.**

Top: **At Colton Junction, Network Rail's Tamper/Liner No DR 73113, a Plasser & Theurer 09-3X-D-RT, runs towards York on 12 February 2013.**

Centre: **Part of the 'business end' of the rail tamper illustrated in the previous picture, which is able to lift the track and pack the ballast, as well as correcting the alignment of the rails to make them parallel and level, thereby reducing wear and giving a smoother ride.**

Bottom: **On display during Railfest 2012 at the National Railway Museum, York, a recent addition to Network Rail's armoury of Track Maintenance Vehicles is seen. This Multi-Purpose Vehicle, No DR 98973 (working with DR 98923) is one of a fleet of 32 two-carriage sets built by the German specialist rolling stock manufacturer Windhoff. Operating nationwide, they can carry various pods for different types of equipment, including rail-head treatment and de-icing fluid.**

Left: **'State-of-the-art' on-track plant in the shape of Network Rail's Harsco Track Technologies RGH-20C Switch & Crossing Rail Grinder, units Nos DR 79271 and DR 79261, work the track between York and Wakefield Kirkgate on 2 April 2013.** ***Rick Ward***

Below: **In the days when track maintenance called for men with shovels, and a steam crane for the really heavy work, Class 08 shunter No 08559 brings in the machinery for a job at York Yard North during August 1979.**

diggers, a common sight on the system until only a few years ago. Rail grinders, for example, are machines that, as they pass over the rails, often during the night, remove irregularities from worn track and thereby restore its profile, so extending its life and improving the ride of trains using the track. They are made by specialist train maintenance companies, which may also operate them under contract.

High-output ballast cleaners, heavy-duty jib cranes and track renewal trains have become essential tools on the modern railway, as have specialist train sets, some hauled by otherwise surplus Class 31, 37, 73 or 86 locomotives, painted in the distinctive 'high visibility' yellow livery. These include 'Track Assessment Trains',

Right: **A track gang work in freezing conditions with machinery including an LNER steam crane, to repair flood damage under the East Coast Main Line near York Yard North on 14 January 1982.**

Above: **Considered very 'high-tech' at the time, a Lab 25 Decapod is in use on the East Coast Main Line near Skelton, north of York, on 11 May 1980. This was developed by BR's Research Division during the 1970s to investigate lateral track forces, curving and rail corrugations. Between the loaded sections is the accommodation for the crew and their instrumentation. It is being hauled by Class 25 No 25254.**

which travel over the entire railway studying track conditions, 'Mobile Load-Bank Locomotives', which draw current from the overhead wire to assess the performance of the power system, and 'Ultra Sonic Test Trains', which use radiographic and eddy-current testing methods as well as ultrasound to check for cracks and flaws in the track. All these are in addition to the more conventional de-icing units, snow ploughs and blowers in use on a seasonal basis.

In recent years a certain amount of criticism, together with a degree of perhaps understandable mockery, has been directed at the railway management's difficulty in coping with seasonal difficulties such as leaf fall and snow on the lines, which can cause lack of adhesion for trains. To combat the autumn leaf fall problem, a set of workings known as Rail Head Treatment Trains (RHTTs) now operate regularly, using a kind of water cannon arrangement to clean the rails.

Undoubtedly the most sophisticated piece of kit in Network Rail's array of maintenance equipment is the New Measurement Train (NMT). Nicknamed the 'Flying Banana', the NMT measures track alignment and monitors the condition of the overhead

Above: **Preserved for posterity, an NER crane stands outside the NRM as an InterCity 125 HST headed by No 254006 passes with an Edinburgh to London King's Cross service on 2 July 1984.**

Right: **When new lengths of track become necessary, the Network Rail track replacement train may be called into action, as seen here, hauled by Class 66 No 66052, in the EWS/DB livery of Euro Cargo Rail at Colton Junction, York, on 15 November 2012.**

An RHTT is seen in operation on the ECML at Colton Junction, York, on 12 October 2012. Two DRS Class 20s, Nos 20301 (at the front) and 20302 are in charge as high-pressure water jets containing 'Sandite', a composite material of sand and aluminium in the form of an adhesive paste, is applied to the rail to aid traction.

In addition to the HSTs in regular service throughout the railway system, Network Rail operates its own set in the form of the New Measurement Train (NMT). This specialised train assesses the condition of the track over which it travels in order to direct engineers to sites in need of attention. The NMT consists of a specially converted HST of two power cars (from the pool of Nos 43013, 43014 and 43062) and a set of Mark 3 coaches packed with sophisticated measuring systems to check all aspects of the track, including geometry, gauge, twist, cant, etc, as it covers most main lines and some secondary routes on a 13-week rolling cycle. Introduced in 2003, its distinctive all-yellow livery has earned it the nickname of the 'Flying Banana'. Headed by No 43013, with No 43014 at the rear, the set passes Colton Junction heading for York on the ECML on 29 June 2013.

On the same day Network Rail's Class 950 track test train No 950001 approaches York from the Leeds direction. This two-car DMU set performs the same functions as the NMT, though concentrating on branch lines where the track quality is not good enough for the larger and heavier assessment vehicles.

wires as it inspects the system at speeds of up to 125mph. It is capable of covering the main inter-city network in just two weeks. Operating continuously on a semi-timetabled basis, the 'Flying Banana' is becoming a familiar sight on our main lines, where its impressive array of monitoring equipment, cameras and associated computing capability have helped move Network Rail from a 'react and repair' to a 'predict and prevent' maintenance regime, as 250,000 miles of infrastructure is monitored and recorded every year.

So as technology continues to become ever more sophisticated, traditional ways of monitoring aspects of railway operation have disappeared, and with them the men who did those jobs. 'Wheel-tappers' are a case in point. These were men employed at large railway stations and goods yards to check the integrity of train wheels by tapping them with a long-handled hammer. A clear bell-like ring indicated that the wheel was 'sound', while a muffled 'clunk' indicated a crack. At the same time, the wheel-tapper would check that the axle-boxes were not excessively hot by using the back of his hand. The wheel-tappers were vital to the smooth running and safety of the railways during and for some time after the Steam Age, but on today's modern network their function is carried out by lineside 'defect detectors', and the wheel-tappers have been consigned to history.

Right: **Hammer in hand, a wheel-tapper walks the length of a train as it pauses at the station during August 1977. A sharp tap on each wheel and a feel of the axle-box will tell him all he needs to know.**

Below centre right: **The modern version is the Phoenix MB Hot Wheel and Hot Box Detection System manufactured by Signal & Systems Technik (SST), whose HQ is at Siershahn near Frankfurt, Germany. Detectors with two infra-red 'eyes' are located on each side of the tracks facing the train's bearings. As they pass over, the detector checks their temperature and if this exceeds the maximum for safe travel (known as a 'hot box') the defect is 'flagged' and the vehicle can no longer continue its journey. Other detectors may be incorporated into the same defect detector location. *'White Cactus'***

Right: **The lengthman of today, part of the Track Maintenance Crew, has at his disposal a wide array of digital technology to assist in monitoring the condition of the track. Here a Network Rail crew member checks the efficiency of the circuits controlling points at Colton Junction near York, on 6 November 2012.**

5. Traction

On a misty 21 February 1975, Class 40 No 40056 takes water at York station with a northbound Liverpool to Newcastle train.

Since 1968 steam traction in the UK has been confined to the blossoming preserved railways and the ever more popular 'charter specials'. Recently, though, we have seen 'heritage diesels' developing a cult following. Together with these main-line diesels, the new electric locos displaced the leviathans and helped bring the Steam Age to what many of us considered to be a premature end, 'outmoded' being a term widely used at the time. Nonetheless, the new age was upon us and the new traction was impressive – and, it had to be admitted, rather exciting. York was yet again a major destination for the new traction, welcoming the ECML expresses and the cross-country trains, and providing shed facilities and stabling for the next generation of workhorses.

Among the first of the main-line express passenger diesel locos were the English Electric 1Co-Co1 Type 4 diesel-electrics. No D200 was the first of the 10 'prototype' Type 4s to become a part of BR stock. It was March 1958, and the deliveries were made to the Eastern Region for acceptance trials at Doncaster. Following these successful trials, a further 190 would be ordered in batches and deployed to upgrade passenger services; the North Eastern Region was allocated 66 locos, the LMR 105 and the Scottish Region 19. The vast majority of these new locos were built at Newton le Willows, home of the Vulcan Foundry works of English Electric, though a small batch of 20, Nos D305 to D324, originated from the Darlington works of Robert Stephenson & Hawthorn (RSH), also by this time a part of English Electric, to allow the Vulcan works the capacity needed to produce the 22 production 'Deltics'. Early examples had provision for intercommunication between locos working in multiple, not uncommon in those days, by the inclusion of access doors in each nose end. These units were fitted with discs and lights for train identification, in the fashion used in steam days, or, as in the case of locos numbered D324 to D344, train indicator boxes on each side of their front ends.

The prefix 'D' was dropped following the end of steam in 1968, and that same year saw the introduction of a new numbering system that incorporated the loco's power rating; thus the Type 4s became Class 40s. Later, in 1973, BR introduced the TOPS computer system and the locos were renumbered in sequence from 40001 to 40199, though D200 was allocated No 40122, as D322 had been withdrawn following its crash at Acton Bridge

Class 40 No 40164 runs northwards down the East Coast Main Line from York, near Shipton by Beningbrough, with an express freight train on 21 July 1975.

in 1966, when it had been hit by runaway wagons on the climb to the Manchester Ship Canal bridge.

The Type 4s had a varied history. Twenty-five carried names on cast brass plates, commemorating famous ocean-going liners that had operated out of Liverpool (an area much served by these locos), though by 1978 it seemed that all of the names had been 'removed'. Early successes for the first batch included working the London-Norwich express services, where they ousted the 'Britannia' 'Pacifics' from the top duties, taking the up 'Flying Scotsman' to Newcastle, and working the 'Sheffield Pullman' and 'Tees-Tyne Pullman', recording running speeds of up to 90mph. On the West Coast route they acquitted themselves well on the 'Caledonian' and 'Royal Scot' services, and also performed admirably over the testing Settle and Carlisle line from Leeds and on diverted West Coast services when necessary. Notoriety of a rather more sinister kind was achieved by No D326, which was the loco involved in the 'Great Train Robbery' of August 1963. Though the class members were used extensively on express passenger services, they were to be replaced as more powerful machines came into production, such as the 'Deltics' on the East Coast Main Line, the electrics on the West Coast route, and the Sulzer Type 4s (Classes 45 and 46) on other passenger turns, with the result that more and more frequently Class 40s were to be seen on heavy freight duties. A notable exception was during the late 1960s through to 1977, when a small fleet of class members were the preferred choice for use on the Royal Train. Such was the case on 1 July 1969 when locos Nos 216 *Campania* and 233 *Empress of England* double-headed the train that carried the Royal Family from Euston to North Wales for the investiture of the Prince of Wales. Thus the Class 40s proved themselves to be versatile machines and regarded as one of the better purchases made by the British Railways Board and its predecessor, the British Transport Commission, and while not being capable of the sustained high-speed running characteristic of their successors, they proved invaluable 'maids of all work' for their operators.

Withdrawals began in the late 1970s as deliveries of Type 5 locos (Classes 56 and 58) proceeded and further dislodged the now aging Class 40s, though some passenger and many freight workings continued well into the 1980s, mainly in the North West and in the Leeds and York areas of Yorkshire. By early 1978 the class was spread between the depots at Longsight, Springs Branch and Kingmoor (LMR); Healey Mills, York and Gateshead (ER); and Haymarket (ScR).

The pioneer loco, No D200, now 40122, was withdrawn from service in August 1981,

Left: **At York MPD on 3 March 1979 Class 40 No 40011 *Mauretania*, now minus nameplates, is stabled in front of Class 47 No 47422.**

Centre left: **No 40030 pauses at York station with an enthusiasts' rail tour, 'The County Durham Crusader', on 17 March 1979.**

Below: **Class 40 No 40153 takes the middle road through York station on 9 July 1979 with a southbound parcels train.**

Left: **No 40058 eases away from a signal check on the East Coast Main Line north of York with a Ribble Cement train heading south on 25 April 1984.**

and though it was hoped, perhaps even expected, that she would immediately become part of the National Collection of preserved locomotives, this turned out not to be the case. It was mainly as a result of a vigorous campaign that she was spared from the scrapyard and restored to full working order, albeit using parts salvaged from a less fortunate sister loco, following a restoration project carried out as part of an apprentice training programme at Toton depot. Restoration completed, D200 re-entered service in April 1983, working in the Carlisle area on duties including a regular return passenger service to Leeds, which generated much-needed publicity for the Settle and Carlisle line at a time when it was threatened with closure. She was also to be seen on special duties such as enthusiasts' rail tours. The surviving 'Whistlers' were withdrawn in January 1985, thereby well outliving the 20-year life expectancy allotted to locomotives by BR's depreciation policy. Four of the class were reinstated in a patched-up condition during April and May of that year to help with freight workings associated with the Crewe station remodelling scheme, finally being withdrawn in 1987. This left D200 as the last of her class still in operation, until she too was withdrawn in April 1988, almost 30 years to the day after first entering service. Fortunately by this time the view of the 'powers that be' had changed, and D200 took her place in the National Collection after all.

The Class 40 Preservation Society had become well established during the final years of the locomotives' working lives, and currently owns two examples of the English Electric Type 4 Class 40, Nos D335 (40135) and D345 (40145), based at Bury on the East Lancashire Railway. As well as these and No D200 there are a further four preserved Class 40s:

- D212/40012 and D213/40013 are housed at the Midland Railway Centre, Butterley, Derbyshire
- D306/40106 is based on the Nene Valley Railway, near Peterborough
- D318/40118 is housed at the Birmingham Railway Museum, Tyseley

The BR Modernisation Plan of 1955 introduced 'dieselisation' in the form of a fascinating variety of locomotives, many of which would disappear under the National Traction Plan of 1967, which was to rationalise locomotive types from 28 down to 15 'standard types'. It would deal the death blow to the diesel-hydraulics and several of the smaller, less successful classes, most of which had been phased out by 1972.

The original 'Peaks', only 10 in number, were introduced in 1959, as British Railways Type 4 1Co-Co1 diesel-electrics, equipped with engines built at Sulzer's Swiss plant and shipped over complete and ready for installation into the locos, which were built at BR's Derby Works. No D1, the first of the class, was outshopped during April 1959 and named *Scafell Pike*, following the plan to name all the locos after British mountains. Even before the trials of the first 'Peaks' were completed, orders were placed for units up to No D147, though perhaps due to a shortage of suitably lofty mountains only the first 10 (later Class 44) received their titles. Later versions were updated and, though still known as 'Peaks', they entered service unnamed, and under the 1968 TOPS classification scheme became Class 45. Some of these were later to be named, taking the names of regiments, in the tradition of the LMS. In all, a further 183 locos were built to the 'Peak' design, the last 56 being designated Class 46.

By 1977, withdrawals of the original 10 Class 44s was well under way. No 44003 *Skiddaw* had gone in August 1976, with No 44010 *Tryfan* a month later. The first of the class, No 44001 *Scafell Pike* was withdrawn in October 1976 and No 44006 *Whernside* in February 1977, leaving just six survivors still in service at that time. The last to be scrapped was No 44 007 *Ingleborough*, at Derby Works in November 1981. Happily, though, two have survived: No 44004 *Great Gable* is preserved at the Midland Railway Trust at Butterley and No 44008 *Penyghent* at Peak Rail, Matlock, Derbyshire. The Class 45 'Peaks', built between 1960 and 1962, became the main traction on the Midland Main Line, successfully accelerating service times from those of the steam era. Though they were relegated to secondary services with the introduction of

HSTs from 1982, they could regularly be seen on long-distance cross-country and trans-Pennine services, such as those between Liverpool and Manchester and Yorkshire and the North East, and doing sterling work over the testing Settle and Carlisle route, until their eventual withdrawal by the end of the 1980s.

Left, top to bottom: **No 45032 heads west from York past Copmanthorpe with a train on the Sheffield route on 7 April 1979.**

Class 45 No 45041 *Royal Tank Regiment* waits at York Yard North on 11 February 1978.

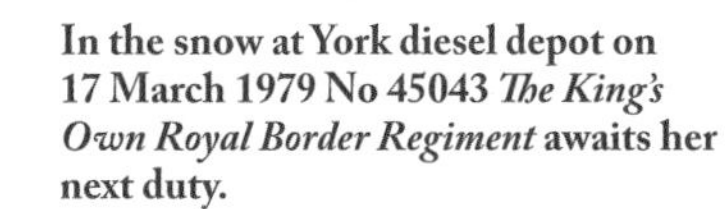

In the snow at York diesel depot on 17 March 1979 No 45043 *The King's Own Royal Border Regiment* awaits her next duty.

Class 45 No 45134 stands at York station with a Plymouth-York excursion on 7 April 1979, as preserved LNER 'V2' No 4771 *Green Arrow* arrives with the Easter steam special 'The Northumbrian Limited'.

Above: **Class 45 nameplates at York station: No 45014 *The Cheshire Regiment*, photographed on 21 February 1975, and No 45006 *Honourable Artillery Company*, on 30 July 1978.**

Above: **A public road alongside the tracks at York MPD allowed easy opportunities to photograph the occupants of the sidings as they awaited their next duties. Here Class 45 No 45039 *The Manchester Regiment* stands nose-to-nose with No 46041.**

Above: **Further across the tracks No 45048 *The Royal Marines* stands in the summer sunshine with No 37019 during August 1979.**

Below: **On 22 October 1984 No 46035 moves into the sidings near the Railway Museum from York station.**

Of the 127 locos produced, 12 have been preserved, three of which are at the Midland Railway Centre, Butterley (Nos 45041 *Royal Tank Regiment*, 45108 and 45133), two at Barrow Hill (Nos 45060 *Sherwood Forester* and 45105), and one each at the Battlefield Line, Mid Hants Railway, FM Rail, Derby Works, East Lancashire Railway, Great Central Railway and Gloucestershire Warwickshire Railway.

The final version of the 'Peak' design, designated Class 46 under TOPS, was built between 1961 and 1963. Originally numbered D138-D193, they were a development of the Class 45, with the same Sulzer engine but fitted with improved Brush generators and traction motors. They too were regular performers on cross-country trains as well as on long-distance freight turns, and in their final days regularly worked the summer Saturday services between the North East, Yorkshire and Lancashire, especially favouring the Newcastle and York to Blackpool trains.

On 17 July 1984 No 46009 was deliberately crashed into a nuclear waste flask at about 90mph on the Old Dalby test track, in a test organised by the CEGB to demonstrate to the public that there would be no leak of radioactive material in the event of a rail accident involving a train carrying such flasks. The locomotive was all but destroyed and

At the National Railway Museum, York, the nuclear waste flask involved in the demonstration crash of 17 July 1984 shows only surface damage. Behind is part of the wreckage of the train.

scrapped on site, but the flask suffered only superficial scratches, and was later displayed to the public at the NRM in York.

Of the 56 locomotives designated Class 46, the first was withdrawn in 1977, and all were gone by 1984. Three of the class have been preserved: Nos 46010, 46035 and D182 (46045).

The prototype 'Deltic', known as DP1, was built by English Electric in 1955, the forerunner of the Class of 22 production locomotives designed to provide the power and speed required to replace Gresley's 'Pacifics' on the Eastern Region. Withdrawn in 1961 following a serious power plant failure, DP1 was donated to the Science Museum, London, and later spent some years adorning the Great Hall of the then newly opened National Railway Museum in York. She now resides at the NRM's 'Locomotion' site in Shildon, County Durham, though a move to the Deltic Preservation Society's headquarters at Barrow Hill is likely in the near future, to enable an engineering survey of the locomotive to be undertaken with the purpose of determining which components still exist. It is not, however, planned to return the loco to operable order.

O. S. Nock, writing in his regular 'British Locomotive Practice and Performance' article for *The Railway Magazine*, turned his attention to the changing nature of express passenger traction in the March 1959 issue. Comparing the performance of the 'new' main-line diesel locomotives with that of the steam 'speedsters' they were to replace, Mr Nock commented on the power generated by the prototype 'Deltic', whose performances were raising eyebrows among seasoned observers of the time. He noted that the total weight of the 'Deltic' was 106 tons, compared to more than 160 tons for an 'A4' 'Pacific' (including tender), about the same for an 'A1' and roughly 150 tons for an 'A3'. This considered, the power-to-weight ratio of the 'Deltic', he observed, 'puts it handsomely in advance of any steam express passenger locomotive now running on British Railways.' He went on to conclude that 'it will be interesting to see what acceleration and improvements of service are possible on the East Coast route when the new Deltics now under construction are in regular service, as they will represent a considerable advance in power over the average capacity of the existing steam Pacifics.'

The 22 production 'Deltics' were built between 1961 and 1962 at English Electric's Vulcan Foundry. Their Napier Deltic two-stroke diesel engine had been designed originally for motor torpedo boats and other Royal Navy craft. The name, from the Greek letter delta, refers to the arrangement of the cylinders in three blocks in a triangular formation, with the crank-cases located at each apex of the triangle. Originally numbered D9000-D9021, later 55001-55022 under TOPS, they were allocated to three depots, Finsbury Park in London, Gateshead and Haymarket in Edinburgh. The Finsbury Park locos were named after famous racehorses – 'Classic' winners like *Meld*, *Alycidon*, *Crepello* and the rest, while the Gateshead and Haymarket units were named after famous regiments. Though they were regarded as temperamental by some, they quickly

The prototype 'Deltic' at the National Railway Museum, York, during August 2001. ***Douglas Todd***

established a reputation as 'something special'. Cecil J. Allen, writing his feature 'Locomotive Running Past and Present' in *Modern Railways* magazine in October 1962, examined the way in which the modern traction of the day could make up lost time. He remarked of the 'Deltics', 'What amazing machines these are,' adding that 'when time has to be made up, it can be done without any strain on the driver's mate, in contrast to what has been the case hitherto with steam power.' Going on to examine logs of early journeys by 'Deltics' between Edinburgh and King's Cross, he concluded, 'We are indeed living in an entirely new realm of locomotive performance.' Even then, in 1962, voices were being heard in support of 'more power'. In the same issue of *Modern Railways*, the editorial feature 'Talking of Trains' argued the case for such advances, pointing out that only by vigorously developing the new technology could rail hope to compete with the motorway or internal air services.

Though the 'Deltics' generated a total of 3,300bhp, it had long been argued by G. F. Fiennes (in *I Tried to Run a Railway* and in 1960s issues of *Modern Railways*) that 4,000hp (and more) was needed to achieve

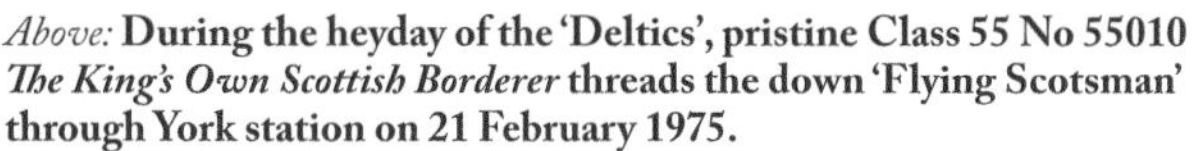

Above: **During the heyday of the 'Deltics', pristine Class 55 No 55010 *The King's Own Scottish Borderer* threads the down 'Flying Scotsman' through York station on 21 February 1975.**

Left: **The nameplate and regimental badge of No 55010 looking rather less pristine at York station on 18 May 1975.**

Below: **On 21 September 1975 No 55021 *Argyll & Sutherland Highlander* brings her train from King's Cross into an unusually quiet York station.**

Above: **The nameplate of No 55021, photographed as she waited at York station on 30 July 1978.**

Right: **No 55020 *Nimbus* takes the northbound 'Aberdonian' away from the station on 21 December 1976.**

commercially competitive speeds. Such 'Super Deltics', including the prospect of a 4,400hp version, continued to be his target. However, it remained a case of 'what might have been' as engineers in the late 1960s continued to wrestle with the problem of how to get more than 3,000hp into what was considered a reliable locomotive. They finally achieved this in 1976, with the Class 56, but what a difference might there have been if Fiennes's case argued in the October 1967 *Modern Railways* had been listened to and acted upon, that the turbocharged 'Deltic' of the design proposed in 1968 could in fact be uprated to 5,000hp in the 1970s, by use of a new engine, lightweight materials and more reliable alternator transmission and solid state circuitry, giving as much power as an HST with 20 tons less dead weight. This achievement would eventually be met by the Class 50s operating north of Crewe – working in multiple!

All that said, the Class 55 'Deltics' were being expertly driven and maintained, with the result that as time went on their admirers increased in number such that they began to achieve almost celebrity status up and down the East Coast Main Line. Railway historian O. S. Nock reviewed the locomotives' achievements in his 'Locomotive Practice and Performance' feature in *The Railway Magazine* of January 1979, and considered that future historians, looking back on the era of diesel-electric locomotive power on the fastest and most important expresses in Great Britain, might well be lost for superlatives in describing their performance. 'Even,' he added, 'when the most glamorous of the East Coast services are being taken over by HST sets, the Deltics are doing better than ever.'

On the East Coast Main Line at Alne, north of York, stable-mates pass at high speed, with No 55018 *Ballymoss* heading south (away from camera) while No 55007 *Pinza* races north on 20 July 1975.

With the reorganisation of motive power depots in the late 1970s, it had been the intention to reallocate all 22 'Deltics' to York for the start of the 1979/80 timetable, but it was later decided that Finsbury Park should keep its allocation, leaving York to receive 14 from Gateshead and Haymarket. At about that time, April 1979, non-specification painting was being applied to No 55003 *Meld* at Finsbury Park depot, in the form of white window surrounds. Perhaps surprisingly, but nonetheless pleasingly, the unofficial paint scheme was accepted by BR's senior hierarchy and soon became the trademark of the Finsbury Park 'Deltics'. Not to be outdone, York depot 'personalised' its 55s by adding the York coat of arms to their paintwork, for which permission had to be granted by the City of York Fathers.

Above: **Racing past Pilmoor, north of York, during August 1979, No 55003 *Meld* sports her 'Finsbury Park' paintwork.**

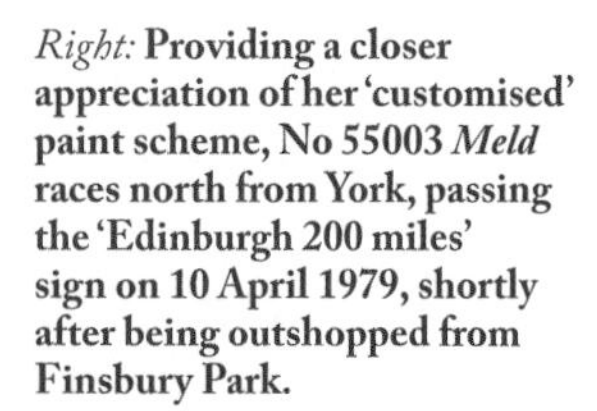

Right: **Providing a closer appreciation of her 'customised' paint scheme, No 55003 *Meld* races north from York, passing the 'Edinburgh 200 miles' sign on 10 April 1979, shortly after being outshopped from Finsbury Park.**

Above: **Passing the same place southbound, No 55011 *The Royal Northumberland Fusiliers* heads for York on 8 June 1980.**

Below: **No 55017 *The Durham Light Infantry* is about to leave King's Cross for the north on 12 April 1981.**

Right: **The nameplate of No 55017, photographed at York station on 18 May 1975.**

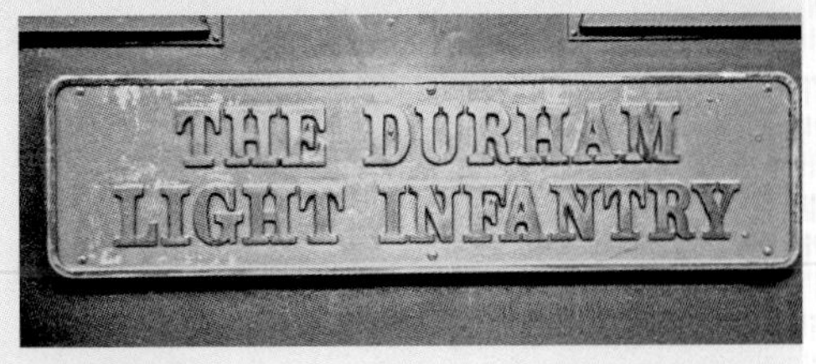

Left: **On 15 April 1975 No 55019 *Royal Highland Fusilier* comes into the platform at King's Cross to take her train to York.**

Top: **Safely attached, No 55019 is almost ready to depart from King's Cross with the 12.20 York train.**

Above: **No 55019's nameplate, photographed at King's Cross.**

Left: **On the same day as the previous photographs, shortly before our York train was due to leave sister loco No 55016 *Gordon Highlander* stormed out of the station into the sunshine with the 12.05 train to Hull.**

Below: **The nameplate and regimental crest of No 55016 at York station on 18 May 1975.**

Meanwhile at the southern end of the East Coast Main Line at London King's Cross the wires were already in place for electric traction, and the 'Deltics' were living on borrowed time. They had dominated ECML express passenger services between London and Edinburgh from their introduction in 1961/62 until 1978, when the Class 43 High Speed Train (HST), branded as 'InterCity 125', was introduced, thus relegating the 'Deltics' to secondary roles. In their final years they were typically run with only limited maintenance until they eventually broke down, usually as a result of engine failure. They would then be taken for scrapping to Doncaster Works, where the 'Deltic scrap line' soon became a 'must visit' location for railway enthusiasts.

Seven withdrawn 'Deltics' sit at Doncaster Works in August 1982. *Black Kite*

Withdrawals began in January 1980, when Nos 55001 *St Paddy* and 55020 *Nimbus* were scrapped. Nos 55003 *Meld* and 55004 *Queen's Own Highlander* were to follow later that year. 1981 saw the end of Nos 55005 *The Prince of Wales's Own Regiment of Yorkshire*, 55006 *The Fife and Forfar Yeomanry*, 55007 *Pinza*, 55010 *The King's Own Scottish Borderer*, 55011 *The Royal Northumberland Fusiliers*, 55012 *Crepello*, 55013 *The Black Watch*, 55014 *The Duke of Wellington's Regiment*, 55017 *The Durham Light Infantry* and 55018 *Ballymoss*.

This left six 'Deltics' that were preserved after their withdrawal: Nos 55022 (originally D9000) *Royal Scots Grey*, 55002 *The King's Own Yorkshire Light Infantry*, 55009 *Alycidon*, 55015 *Tulyar*, 55016 *Gordon Highlander* and 55019 *Royal Highland Fusilier*. In addition, one cab has been preserved from each of Nos 55008 *The Green Howards* and 55021 *Argyll & Sutherland Highlander*, both on display at the Deltic Preservation Society (DPS) depot at Barrow Hill, 'Britain's last surviving working roundhouse', Staveley, Chesterfield.

On 28 November 1981 two novel rail tours were organised to commemorate the demise of the Class 55s in BR service. 'The Deltic Venturer' was organised by the Severn Valley Railway Society to run from York to Paddington via Derby, Birmingham, Swindon and Reading, returning via the Cotswold line to Oxford, then Worcester and up the Lickey Incline to Birmingham before heading back to York by way of Sheffield, with No 55022 *Royal Scots Grey* in charge. 'The Deltic Devonian' featured No 55016 *Gordon Highlander*, sponsored by BR and run from Finsbury Park on a circular route to the Western Region by way of Slough, Newbury, Taunton and Exeter, then returning via Yeovil, Salisbury, Basingstoke, Woking and Clapham Junction. This involved journeys over routes on which the class was previously unknown and therefore necessitated the addition of a conductor-driver, whose advice would be essential if these temperamental and by now fairly run-down locomotives were to be negotiated successfully over unfamiliar routes.

By the January 1982 issue of *The Railway Magazine*, 'Locomotive Practice and Performance' had been taken over by P. W. B. Semmens, following O. S. Nock's retirement with the December 1980 feature after 22 years in the job. His theme was 'Farewell to the Deltics', in which he bemoaned the fact that within a couple of weeks of that issue's publication the East Coast route would no longer throb to the exhaust note of the 'Deltics', as the 21-year reign of what was the world's most powerful diesel locomotive would be at an end. He noted that back in 1967 Gerry Fiennes had written, 'I never hear the high full-throated thrum of a Deltic without returning thanks to the people in English Electric who thought of putting an engine off a Motor Gunboat into a locomotive.'

Peter Semmens went on to observe that in the course of running a total of some 64 million miles, the 'Deltics' had served the public very well indeed, and added his own personal lament by explaining that his home in York was less than half a mile from the main line, and 'it is sad to think that next summer it will no longer be possible to lie in bed and hear through the open window the characteristic beat of a Deltic as it opens up to accelerate its sleeping cars northwards out of the station.'

My last 'working Deltic' was No 55007 *Pinza*, which was in charge of the 10.05 'stopper' from King's Cross to York. The date was 27 December 1981, and conditions were freezing, with snow on the ground (even in London!). Knowing that the survivors had but a few days left made this journey all the more poignant, though it was probably more memorable for most of the passengers because it was endured throughout with no train heating! What a chilling and inglorious end to my 'Deltic Days'.

In fact, the last scheduled 'Deltic'-hauled train to run was the 16.30 Aberdeen to York service on 31 December 1981, taken from Edinburgh by No 55019 *Royal Highland Fusilier*, with 2 January 1982 being the date set for the finale of the Class 55s. The route was to be the classic one – King's Cross to Edinburgh and return – with Mark 1 stock and fast timings. This last run, 'The Deltic Scotsman Farewell', was set to feature green-liveried No 55002 *The King's Own Yorkshire Light Infantry* for the northbound run and erstwhile Haymarket loco No 55022 *Royal Scots Grey* southbound. However, No 55002 had failed earlier in the week and been withdrawn, to be replaced by former Finsbury Park 'racehorse' No 55015 *Tulyar*, resplendent with white cab surrounds of course!

The tour proved a great success, with both locos acquitting themselves admirably, making light of the 90mph running, more than 785 miles there and back, and a heavy load of 20-to-30-year-old coaches, described in the April 1982 issue of *Railway World* as 'a fitting finale – a farewell … not just to the Deltics, but to East Coast locomotive-hauled trains, and the sort of Inter-City trains that paved the way for so much.'

Waiting in the snow at King's Cross with the 10.05 train to York on 27 December 1981 is No 55007 *Pinza*, my last 'Deltic' working in BR service.

Where are they at the time of writing?

- No D9000 (55022) *Royal Scots Grey* now resides at Bury on the East Lancashire Railway. It is certified for main-line running and carries the City of York coat of arms above its numbers.
- D9002 (55002) *The King's Own Yorkshire Light Infantry*, also certified for main-line working, is housed at the National Railway Museum, York.
- D9009 (55009) *Alycidon* was purchased by the Deltic Preservation Society (DPS) and is based at the society's depot at Barrow Hill.
- D9015 (55015) *Tulyar* is also owned by the DPS and has been on loan to several heritage railways.
- D9016 (55016) *Gordon Highlander* is also based on the East Lancashire Railway.
- D9019 (55019) *Royal Highland Fusilier* is also owned and operated by the DPS.

The DPS locos were made available to heritage railways from their early days in preservation, and No 55009, together with No 55019, could be seen on the North Yorkshire Moors Railway during the 1980s.

Right: **At Grosmont on the North Yorkshire Moors Railway on 30 October 1982, No 55009 *Alycidon* is passed by Type 2 Class 24/0 Bo-Bo No D5032 (24032) with a train for Pickering.**

Below: **Stabled on shed outside Grosmont station on 30 August 1984 are 'Deltics' Nos 55009 *Alycidon* and 55019 *Royal Highland Fusilier*.**

Below right: **The year 2011 was the 50th birthday of the remaining 'Deltics', and five of their number were gathered together at Shildon and on the East Lancashire Railway to celebrate. On 11 October, led by No 55022 *Royal Scots Grey*, the five locos leave Shildon and head for Bury, on the East Lancashire Railway, to celebrate their 50th birthday.**

Left: **A week later, on 18 October, No 55022 leads No 55002 *The King's Own Yorkshire Light Infantry* back to the NRM at York through Colton Junction, before itself returning light engine to Bury. Job done!**

Below: **Those surviving Class 55 'Deltics' with main-line certification are kept busy with rail tour bookings as well as their 'guest appearances' on heritage railways. Here No 55022 *Royal Scots Grey*, with No 57601 in tow, takes Spitfire Railtour's Worcester to Edinburgh tour 'The Scotsman' north from York in the early morning sunshine of 29 November 2011.**

Less than a week later, on 2 December 2011, No 55022 was in action again on the main line, heading south for Lincoln with SRPS Railtours' 'The Santa Express' through Colton Junction, York.

6. The 'Golden Age' of diesels

For many, therefore, the 1950s and '60s represented the 'Golden Age' of the diesels. It was a time during which rapid progress in terms of power output, speed and reliability on inter-city passenger duties saw steam traction replaced throughout the network and condemned to scrap, or relegated to private collections and the embryonic 'heritage railways'. The most numerous of the British main-line diesels were the Brush Type 4s (later Class 47), of which 512 were built between 1962 and 1968 at BR's Crewe Works and at Brush's Falcon Works at Loughborough. The locomotives proved highly successful on both express passenger and freight duties throughout the country, and played a large part in the process of replacing the aging steam fleet. As such, they engendered mixed emotions among railway enthusiasts. Originally numbered D1100 to D1111 and D1500 to D1999, they were later reclassified into sub-classes and renumbered in the range 47001 to 47981.

Above: **Class 47/4 No 47431 hurries north near Pilmoor on the fast stretch of the ECML between York and Northallerton on 10 August 1975 with a King's Cross-Edinburgh express.**

Left: **Sister loco No 47471 approaches Northallerton station, on the ECML north of York, with a train for the south on 20 August 1975.**

Within the splendid arched roof of York station in January 1981, Class 47/4 No 47508 *Great Britain* waits to take her train on to Scotland.

An early example of a named Class 47 was No 47083 *Orion*, photographed on 21 February 1975, while the nameplate of No 47404 *Hadrian* is seen on 12 April 1982, both at York station.

By the time the 1980s were under way, the much-loved tradition of 'naming' locomotives had returned to favour among the powers that be in the railway establishment, and as time progressed so did the number and variety of names chosen to adorn our locomotives. During the 1970s fewer than 20 of the Class 47s bore a name; by the early 1980s the total had risen to more than 50 and continued to climb as the practice gained popular support.

The first withdrawals of 'life-expired' Class 47s began in 1986, these being from the original non-standard batch of 20; by 1992 all 20 had gone. Between 1996 and 2006 an average of about 15 locos per year were taken out of service, and this process continues to the present day, so that by 2012 only about 30 locomotives were still in operation on the national network. These were being operated by such companies as the national railfreight operator Direct Rail Services (DRS), which was running eight, West Coast Railways had 21, nine of which were operational, Riviera Trains had six, Colas Rail three, and Nemesis Rail one.

In addition, 34 of the class have been preserved to operate on heritage railways up and down the country, including the Midland Railway Trust at Butterley, the East Lancashire Railway, the Embsay & Bolton Abbey Railway, the Great Central Railway, the Eden Valley Railway, the West Somerset Railway, the Gloucestershire Warwickshire Railway, the Mid Norfolk Railway, the North Norfolk Railway, the Wensleydale Railway, the Colne Valley Railway, and at the National Railway Museum in York. Included among these 'survivors' are the one-time Royal Train locomotives, Nos 47798 (now named *Prince William* and part of the National Collection) and 47799 (*Prince Henry*). These and other classmates are regular performers on charter specials over the main lines, either hauling tours in their own right or acting as back-up on steam-hauled excursions.

In addition to the Class 47s that are still operational, either for main-line duties or on heritage railways, a further 33 of those withdrawn were subsequently rebuilt and reclassified as Class 57. These locos work passenger trains for First Great Western and Virgin Trains, as well as freight for the goods company Freightliner. The prototype passenger loco for this class, No 57001, is operated by West Coast Railways based at Carnforth MPD, together with sister locos Nos 57601 (operational) and 57005 and 57006 (under repair), as part of the company's fleet that includes Class 47s mentioned earlier, Class 37s and Class 33s.

In September 1993 Class 47 No 47618 is seen at Bradford station after having brought in the first leg of a charter from York to Carlisle. The remainder of the tour over the magnificent Settle and Carlisle route was headed by preserved Gresley 'A4' No 4498 *Sir Nigel Gresley*. No 47618, in common with many of her class, has appeared in various guises during her long career. Introduced into traffic on 11 August 1964 as No D1609, she was renumbered first to 47030 in December 1973, then to 47618 in August 1984. On 11 September 1984 she received the name *Fair Rosamund* from sister loco No 47510 (when that loco was converted to Class 47/7 No 47713). However, the name was not retained when she in turn was converted and renumbered to 47836 in August 1989. This was not to be the end of the saga, however, as in April 1993 she was again renumbered – back to 47618 – until in January 1994 she became 47780, the number she was to carry until being finally withdrawn and cut up on 7 August 2007.

In more recent times the preserved Class 47s have been regular performers on special excursions and charter trains, their reputation for reliability ensuring that they are constantly in demand to work even the longest and most challenging of rail tours. One such is the luxurious 'Northern Belle', which entered service in 2000 offering what its operators describe as 'the ultimate in stylish day excursions and short breaks'. Combining the opulence of the English 1930s 'Belle' trains with the elegance of the Pullman carriages of the 'Venice-Simplon Orient Express', these trains depart from regional stations throughout the UK and provide passengers with a journey

Class 47 No 47832 *Solway Princess* heads the 'Northern Belle' away from York on 14 October 2011, passing Shipton by Beningbrough as she races northwards. Built at BR Crewe Works and introduced into traffic on 13 August 1964 as No D1610, later to become 47031, then 47560 and be named *Tamar*, she retained the name when renumbered again to 47832 on 19 June 1989. On 11 September 2005 she was renamed *Driver Tom Clark OBE* at Crewe Works Open Day, only to be renamed again at Crewe Gresty Bridge Open Day on 19 July 2008 when she became *Solway Princess*. She is seen here running in the DRS 'Northern Belle' livery with train 1Z90, from Leeds to Edinburgh and return.

Left: **Sister loco No 47790 *Galloway Princess* brings the 'Northern Belle' through Poppleton station, between Harrogate and York, on 16 February 2012. Also built at Crewe Works and entering service on 10 November 1965 as No D1973, she later became 47272, then 47593 when she was named *Galloway Princess*. She retained the name when reclassified to Class 47/6 and renumbered again to 47673, but was later to be renamed *York Inter City Control* at York station on 22 March 1994. This name lasted only a year, as on 1 March 1995 she was yet again renumbered, at Swansea High Street station, this time to 47790, and given the name *Saint David/Dewi Sant*, the name previously carried by No 47600. However, all was restored on 11 July 2009 at the DRS Open Day held at the company's Carlisle Kingmoor Depot headquarters, when she was renamed *Galloway Princess* once more, and repainted in the DRS 'Northern Belle' livery of crimson lake and cream.**

Left: **Preserved ex-Royal Train loco No 47798 *Prince William* races northwards from York past Shipton by Beningborough with a shuttle between the NRM's York and Shildon museums on 18 September 2011. Another Crewe-built loco, this one entered service on 1 February 1965 as No D1656, to become 47072 from January 1974 and 47609 from April 1984, then being named *Fire Fly* in August 1985. The name was retained when she was renumbered to 47834 in July 1989, but the plates were removed in March 1995 prior to the loco being again renumbered 47798 and renamed *Prince William*. The loco also carries the 'ER' crest and 'Royal Livery', was preserved from August 2004, and is based at the NRM, York.**

through the best of British landscapes to visit cities, castles and major events, the passengers being wined and dined in fine surroundings.

The English Electric Co-Co Type 4 diesel-electrics, later Class 50, were introduced from 1967. Originally leased to BR and numbered D400-D449, many were later refurbished, and all 50 were named, the nameplates being added gradually over a period of months from the beginning of 1978 as the locos entered Doncaster Depot for maintenance. The fleet was titled the 'Warship' Class, evoking memories of the earlier Western Region diesel-hydraulic class of the same name, the last of which had been withdrawn in 1972.

These new 'Warships' entered service on the West Coast Main Line, working express passenger trains on the yet to be electrified section north from Crewe, taking over from the electric locomotives that had worked the trains out of London Euston. The steep gradients of Shap and Beattock over which the line runs to Glasgow meant that these trains often needed to be double-headed by the Class 50s, a practice that brought the advantage of increasing the reliability of the original build locos, which suffered a high failure rate. A joke among train crews at the time was that these pairings would only have a '50-50' chance of completing the journey with no failures. Many of the breakdowns were attributed to problems with their inertial air filter systems, which were to be improved in later refurbishments. These modifications eliminated the characteristic 'sucking' noise that had led enthusiasts to refer to the locos as 'Hoovers', though the nickname was to remain with them throughout their lives.

The first of the class to be withdrawn from service was in early 1987, when No 50011 *Centurion* departed, closely followed that year by Nos 50006 *Neptune* and 50014 *Warspite*. Next to go were Nos 50010 *Monarch*, 50013 *Agincourt*, 50022 *Anson*, 50038 *Formidable* and 50047 *Swiftsure*, all scrapped during 1988. Though some consideration was given to modifying the Class 50s for freight duties, trials showed them to be less than ideal for that role, so by the early 1990s the decision was taken to retire the rest of the fleet. By 1992 only eight remained in service (Nos 50007 *Hercules*, 50008 *Thunderer*, 50015 *Valiant*, 50029 *Renown*, 50030 *Repulse*, 50033 *Glorious*, 50046 *Ajax* and 50050 *Fearless*), and during the 1990s several 'farewell' rail tours were organised to commemorate the run-down of the fleet, culminating in 1994 with No 50033 running to the National Railway Museum for preservation as part of the National Collection, and Nos 50007 and 50050 running a tour between London's Waterloo station and Penzance. Both of these locos were later also preserved. In fact, such was the popularity of the class that in total 18 of its members have been saved for preservation, several being registered for main-line working. The Severn Valley Railway has four of the class in its stock, all operational, and two main-line registered; Tyseley Loco Works has two, as have Peak Rail and the East Lancashire Railway; while others can be found as far afield as the North Yorkshire Moors Railway, the Mid Norfolk Railway and the Bodmin & Wenford Railway.

On the approach to York from the north at Clifton Sidings, Class 50 No 50007 *Hercules* brings in her train during August 1979.

The preserved Class 50s are Nos 50002 *Superb*, 50007 *Hercules* (renamed *Sir Edward Elgar* at the Midland Railway Trust, Butterley, on 25 February 1984), 50008 *Thunderer*, 50015 *Valiant*, 50017 *Royal Oak*, 50019 *Ramillies*, 50021 *Rodney*, 50026 *Indomitable*, 50027 *Lion*, 50029 *Renown*, 50030 *Repulse*, 50031 *Hood*, 50033 *Glorious*, 50035 *Ark Royal*, 50042 *Triumph*, 50044 *Exeter*, 50049 *Defiance* and 50050 *Fearless*.

Perhaps the accolade of 'the last main-line diesel passenger locomotive built and operated on our

On display at the NRM, York, on 8 November 2012 is preserved Class 50 No 50008 *Thunderer*.

network' should belong to the Class 57s. Strictly speaking, though, as already mentioned these 33 locomotives were not new, but were rebuilt by Brush Traction at Loughborough between 1997 and 2004 from redundant Class 47s. They are fitted with refurbished engines and reconditioned alternators to improve reliability and performance, and occur in three variants. Subclass 57/0, of which there are 12, is the freight train variant, while subclass 57/3 (numbering 16) and subclass 57/6 (five) are designed for passenger services. The locos are currently operated by Direct Rail Services, First Great Western, Network Rail, Virgin Trains and Colas Rail.

Above left: **Class 57/3 No 57309 in Direct Rail Services 'Compass' livery is shown off alongside Class 56 No 56312 at York on 5 June during Railfest 2012.**

Left: **At the same event was Class 57 No 57604. As described in the text, the Class 57s, introduced by Brush Traction between 1997 and 2004, are rebuilds of former Class 47 locos, with reconditioned engines. No 57604 was rebuilt from No 47209. Named *Pendennis Castle*, she is owned by First Great Western and is seen here outshopped in GWR 'Brunswick**

West Coast Railways also operates the prototype Class 57/6 No 57601, which it uses on its charter trains, painted in WCR maroon livery to match its coaching stock. WCR also owns three examples from Class 57/0, Nos 57001, 57005 and 57006. Their re-engineered nature within an earlier body shell has earned them nicknames such as 'Body-snatchers' and 'Zombies' among enthusiasts.

The introduction of the prototype High Speed Train (HST) in 1972 signalled the beginning of the end for single-unit diesel passenger locomotives on the British rail network. Though themselves originally considered to be composed of two locos, one at each end of a rake of carriages, they were soon to be reclassified as diesel multiple units (DMUs). This accounts for the confusing numbering schemes seen on early HST sets, as the power cars were first designated Class 41, then as DMUs to Class 252. Only two power cars were built as Class 41s, Nos 41001 (which is preserved at the National Railway Museum, York) and 41002 (which was scrapped in 1990), though at the reclassification these had been given the coaching stock numbers 43000 and 43001. Thus the prototype power car preserved at York bears the numbers 43000 and 252001.

After successfully completing trials on the Eastern Region, the prototype was transferred to the Western Region where it operated on Paddington to Bristol and Weston-super-Mare services. This initial success led to orders being placed for a further 197 power cars to operate on the Western, Eastern, London Midland and Scottish regions, while the prototype unit itself was withdrawn. These new power cars were designated Class 43 and numbered 43002 to 43198. They were powered by Paxman Valenta engines giving a regular running speed in service of 125mph and an absolute maximum speed of 148mph, making them the fastest diesel locomotives in the world.

When introduced from 1975 and designated Classes 253 and 254, the 253 sets operated on BR Western Region and on cross-country trains, while the 254 sets ran on the Eastern and Scottish regions. The power cars continued to carry their diesel locomotive Class 43 numbers, though in some cases the Class 253 or 254 number was also displayed, and the units were collectively known as 'InterCity 125' sets. A total of 95 sets were built between 1975 and 1982.

The December 1976 issue of *The Railway Magazine* heralded the introduction of the first accelerated schedules on the Paddington to Bristol and South Wales lines, the services using the newly delivered HST sets. While noting that only 80 miles of the route had so far been cleared for 125mph running, it was evident that the new schedules were among the fastest in the world for which diesel traction was responsible, and thus introduced 'a new dimension of speed to British Railways'. In his 'Locomotive Practice and Performance' article for the March 1977 issue of the magazine, O. S. Nock not only hailed the new HST services to date as a great success, but went on to observe that the 'sparkling performances' of the HST

Green' livery. HST sets pass at Pilmoor, on the fast stretch of the East Coast Main Line north of York, on 21 May 1978. No 254006 races north (towards the camera) while No 254007 heads south.

sets 'seem to have had a stimulating effect on express train running generally between Paddington and Bristol,' citing logs of spirited runs behind Class 50 locos with trains not yet furnished with the new improved coaching stock.

Working on the East Coast Main Line at Shipton by Beningbrough, north of York, an HST set headed by No 254011 heads south with an Edinburgh to King's Cross service on 10 July 1978.

No 254018 brings the northbound 'Flying Scotsman' through York station on 24 July 1978.

Mr Nock had similar praise for the performances of the HST sets and their crews following their introduction on ECML workings. In his article in *The Railway Magazine* of June 1980 he noted the consistency achieved in running times, often in spite of speed restrictions, with 100mph-plus being logged on a regular basis and 125mph frequently being achieved on the fast stretches such as between Grantham and Peterborough and between York and Northallerton.

BR's investment in and commitment to the HST programme was illustrated by P. W. B. Semmens's article in *The Railway Magazine* of February 1983. Having succeeded O. S.

An HST set headed by No 254007 gets the green light and takes the 15.34 service from York, the King's Cross to Edinburgh service, on 24 February 1979.

Nock as author of 'Locomotive Practice and Performance' feature, he noted that the HSTs formed 20% of InterCity's resources for moving people, yet they were running no less than 40% of its train miles, and that under current plans this would be increased to 55%. Quite a challenging objective, Mr Semmens observed, and one that would depend for its success as much on the utilisation of the sets themselves as on their scheduling, as their range increased to include the North East-South West cross-country route and the Midland Main Line out of St Pancras.

Right: **Contrasts at Clifton Junction, York, as preserved Gresley 'A4' No 4498 *Sir Nigel Gresley* brings in the 'Yorkshire Circular' rail tour from the Harrogate branch, while HST power car No 254005 is at the rear of a King's Cross to Edinburgh train on 8 July 1979.**

More than three decades after their introduction, the majority of the HST fleet is still operating successfully over much of the network, from Penzance to Inverness, though the power cars now have new engines and the coaches have been refurbished. The final runs involving an HST power car fitted with the original Valenta engine took place on 22 December 2010, when No 43123 hauled two return 'specials' between Sunderland and York.

Above: **On 18 July 1994 'Intercity 125' HST No 43195 rolls into York with an Edinburgh to King's Cross service.**

Top left: **Journey No 1 of 4 on 22 December 2010. Grand Central's HST power car No 43468, with No 43123 at the rear, approaches York from Sunderland, passing Shipton by Beningbrough.**

Centre left: **Preparing for what was to be the last ever run of an HST powered by its original Valenta engine before the power unit was replaced by the new MTU version, No 43123 poses for enthusiasts at York station.**

Left: **Now an hour late due to a signal failure north of the station, sole Valenta-engined survivor No 43123 prepares to leave for Sunderland with Journey 4. The last one!**

Above: **The commemorative nameplate carried by No 43123, as seen at York station on 22 December 2010.**

After having its Paxman Valenta engine replaced by the MTU 'upgrade', and subsequently being renumbered 43423, *Valenta 1972-2010* was back in action again on the ECML speeding north from York at the rear of this Grand Central service to Newcastle, headed by No 43484, on 8 November 2012.

As a result of the Railways Act of 1993, which brought about the privatisation of British Rail, the new train operating companies painted the HSTs in their own colour schemes. In the South West of England and South Wales, HSTs are operated by First Great Western, in Eastern England and Scotland by GNER, National Express, East Coast Railways and the Grand Central Railway Company, and on the former London Midland Region by East Midlands Trains, while Virgin Trains and Arriva operate cross-country HST services, in addition to those over the West Coast route and in the North Wales area.

Left: **On the East Coast Main Line near Shipton by Beningbrough, north of York, an East Coast Railways' HST set headed by power car No 43317 heads for the north on 18 May 2012.**

Below left: **Cross Country Trains' HST No 43366 powers away from York past Bolton Percy on 31 August 2012.**

Below: **Approaching York at Colton Junction on 1 December 2012 is an East Midlands Trains HST set forming 1Z43, the St Pancras-Kettering-York 'St Nicholas Fayre in York' special tour, led by No 43043 with No 43081 at the rear.**

Left: **Grand Central's HST set, with No 43484 at the head, pauses at York with a Newcastle to King's Cross service on 18 January 2013.**

Below: **The nameplate of No 43484.**

As the long-serving HST fleet is now in its fourth decade, a replacement is being actively sought, with the building and testing of possible successors already under way, led by the Department for Transport. A consortium headed by Hitachi will design a Super Express Train in various formations, including an electric and bi-modal diesel-electric version. In the meantime, high-speed DMUs such as the Bombardier 'Voyager' family and the Alstom Class 180 'Zephyrs' have replaced some services, but increasing demand has forced all HST sets back into service.

Above: **Cross Country Trains Class 221 'Super Voyager' set No 221133 passes Bolton Percy heading for York on 31 August 2012.**

Left: **Another 'HST replacement', in the shape of Grand Central's Class 180 'Zephyr' set No 180114, approaches York on the ECML near Shipton by Beningbrough on 8 June 2013.**

7. The early diesel freight locomotives

The early use of diesel shunters was pioneered by the LMS with its prototype No 1831 built in 1931 from the remains of a former Midland Railway '1377' Class 0-6-0T steam loco of 1892 vintage. Though less than a roaring success, and indeed withdrawn only eight years later, it nevertheless provided the basis for a radical rethink of the design of small shunting locos. The 1930s saw several developments based on the lessons learned from No 1831, a number of which passed into service with the War Department and, after the second World War, went to work with BR or industrial users such as the National Coal Board.

From the early 1950s BR commissioned a series of 0-4-0 and 0-6-0 diesel-mechanical shunters, often in tiny numbers, from a variety of manufacturers. These were Class 01 and 02 locos, the forerunners of the more successful Classes 03 and 04, which would themselves rapidly evolve into the highly acclaimed designs of later years. Manufacturers of these early designs included Drewry, Barclay, Hudswell-Clarke, Hunslet, North British, the Yorkshire Engine Company and Ruston & Hornsby. Locos were also supplied directly to industrial users operating short lines with tight curves, for which these designs proved ideal. Many dockside, colliery and mining companies bought the locos, as did large organisations such as the British Sugar Corporation (BSC).

A case in point was BSC's York works, adjacent to the ECML at York Yard North, with access at Skelton Junction, from where BR would deliver molasses and carry away refined sugar from the Corporation's sidings, being handled within the property by BSC's own shunters. Ruston & Hornsby (R&H) 0-4-0 Class DS No 165, Works No 395304, was York's resident loco for many years. Built at Lincoln in 1956 for British Sugar, she worked at the York factory until BSC ceased moving materials by rail and concentrated on road haulage. Before that, she was joined by a sister loco, built in 1953 to Works No 327964, and transferred from BSC's Selby factory when it closed in 1981. Two of this type were purchased by BR in 1956, Class DY1 Nos 11507 and 11508, renumbered from 1958 as BR Class D1/3 Nos D2957 and D2958; they spent most of their working lives at Stratford, East London, until sold in 1967, one to industry, the other for scrap. The lucky survivor was D2957, which was later fully restored and now adorns the stock list of the Severn Valley Railway, together with R&H sister locos from the company's Lincoln Works, Nos D2960 *Silver Spoon* (Works No 281260, built 1950) and D2961 (Works No 418596, built 1957). D2957 has also appeared on the Epping & Ongar Railway in Essex.

Another example, Works No 327974, which had been built for BSC's Bardney factory in Lincolnshire in 1954 (at a price of £8,213), was later transferred to the Corporation's works at King's Lynn, Norfolk, in 1982. After spending some time there, No 327974 was acquired by the Great Eastern Traction Group for use

Ruston & Hornsby 0-4-0 shunter, Works No 395304, stands in the yard at BSC's York factory, with Selby 'transfer', Works No 327964, in the background.

at Hardingham station, Norfolk. From there it went on to the Northampton Ironstone Railway Trust at Hunsbury Hill, Northampton. Finally, in 2007, the shunter, together with sister loco Works No 395305, was purchased by the Helston Railway for use at its Trevarno headquarters in Cornwall.

Even though in 1958 the end of steam was still 10 years away, the process of 'dieselisation' was progressing with what many considered 'undue haste', as new classes of passenger and freight locomotives were introduced on our railways. Among the earliest introductions, dating from 1934, had been the English Electric 350/400bhp 0-6-0 diesel-electric shunters, later widely known as Class 08, which began to replace their steam equivalents from 1953, as did the subsequent freight classes that appeared in the late 1950s and early 1960s.

The Class 08 diesel-electric shunters were built at BR's works at Crewe, Derby, Doncaster, Darlington and Horwich, mainly between 1953 and 1962, and came to number 996 locomotives, making them the most numerous of all British locomotive classes. They became BR's general-purpose shunter, to be found working where any shunting job was required, and becoming a familiar sight in goods yards and stations the length and breadth of the network. When the outwardly very similar Class 09 and Class 10

Above left: **No 327964 receives attention on 10 October 1992. Both this loco and No 395304 were built new for British Sugar, so never worked on BR. No 395304 was later to be scrapped, while No 327964 was preserved and is now operational on the Derwent Valley Light Railway in York. BSC closed its York factory in 2007 and it was later demolished.**

Left: **Still going strong and working at Holgate Junction on 2 July 1984 is BR Class 03 0-6-0 shunter No 03089, one of 200 such locos introduced from 1957. By 2013 no fewer than 56 members of this successful class had survived into preservation. One example, No 03179, is still operational on the network, owned by the train operating company First Capital Connect and employed on shunting duties at the company's Hornsey depot in North London.**

locos were included, the count rose to 1,193 in total. In fact, many small variations existed within the basic design, but so successful was the concept that oversees customers also bought them in considerable numbers, notably the Netherlands, where 125 found a new home, making them that country's standard shunting locomotive. Further orders came from Egypt, Sweden, Malaya, Sudan and Australia, while at home many were employed by industrial users on their own rail systems, including the National Coal Board, quarry owners and dock companies, bringing the grand total built between 1934 and 1962 to 1,278 locomotives, making the 0-6-0 diesel-electric a good candidate for not only the British, but possibly the world title of 'largest numerical class'.

By 1967 the process of withdrawing and scrapping the 08s had begun and was to accelerate through the 1970s and 1980s, until by the early 1990s most of their vast number were gone. But not all, as more than 60 examples have been given a second lease of life working successfully on our heritage railways, and a similar number still survive to ply their trade on private industrial sidings.

The English Electric Type 1 Bo-Bos, later Class 20, were introduced from 1957, initially as light freight locos, but they soon came to be used in pairs, mainly in the Midlands on coal trains, though they were also to be seen almost anywhere on the network. A total of 228 were built at the Vulcan Foundry and at RSH between 1957 and 1968. Though they were occasionally used on passenger services, the limited visibility for the driver when

Above: **A permanent way gang checks the track at York Yard North during August 1979, while beyond them Class 08 shunter No 08245 moves a rake of wagons out of the sidings.**

Below: **Diesel shunter No 08567 is seen in BR blue livery at York. Now owned by DB Schenker, she has joined so many other surplus locos in store for parts at that company's Traction Maintenance Depot at Toton, Nottinghamshire. *Rick Ward***

being driven nose-first did create problems (though no more so than with the steam locos they replaced), so 'doubling up' overcame this difficulty while at the same time increasing their pulling power.

In more recent times, the Class 20s have proved popular with heritage railways, with no fewer than 26 of the class having been preserved, including the class pioneer, No D8000 (TOPS No 20050), which is now part of the National Collection based at the National Railway Museum in York. Others have found new homes at such venues as the Great Central Railway (Nos 20007 and 20098), the Keighley & Worth Valley Railway (20031), the Severn Valley Railway (20059, 20117 and 20188), the East Lancashire Railway (20087), the North Norfolk Railway (20118), the Gloucestershire Warwickshire Railway (20137), and the Wensleydale Railway (20166).

The National Railway Museum's 08 shunter, No 08911 *Matey*, is seen on display at York on 5 June during Railfest 2012.

Introduced in the same year, 1957, were the Class 31s, known at the time as Brush Type 2s. A total of 263 Class 31s were built between 1957 and 1962 to replace steam traction, originally for use on the Eastern Region. However, once fitted with the more powerful English Electric engines from 1964, they became a frequent sight on the Western and London Midland regions as well. The first batch of 20, designated Class 31/0 and numbered D5500-D5519, were allocated to East Anglian sheds, as were many of the second generation, or Class 31/1s (numbered 31101-31327). However, they also found homes at Finsbury Park, Tinsley, Immingham and Thornaby on the Eastern Region, as well as Bristol Bath Road and Old Oak Common on the Western Region, and at Healey Mills and Bescot on the London Midland Region, where they were to replace Class 25s.

The later Class 31/4s, numbered 31400 to 31469, were modified 31/1s, to which Electric Train Heating (ETH) had been fitted but, because of the power needed to run the ETH, that remaining for traction was considerably reduced, meaning that only short passenger trains could be operated and therefore use and performance were severely

Class 20 Nos 20201 and 20054 work in unison on the East Coast Main Line north of York near Beningbrough, taking their partially fitted freight train northwards on 12 August 1975.

restricted. Some of the class saw service with the commercial operators English, Welsh & Scottish (EWS), FM Rail, Mainline Rail and Network Rail, and more than 30 locos were purchased for preservation by heritage railways, though some have subsequently been scrapped.

The first-built, No D5500 (later 31108), was withdrawn in 1976 and is now part of the National Collection, while No D5862 (31327), the last to be built, now operates on the Strathspey Railway. Other locations for preserved 31s include the Nene Valley, Dean Forest, Embsay & Bolton Abbey, North Norfolk, Mid Norfolk and Great Central railways.

The late 1950s and early 1960s were a busy time for railway locomotive builders, as the race to replace steam traction gained momentum. Large deliveries of both freight and passenger locos were needed, and the English Electric Co-Co Type 3s, later to be known as Class 37, were produced in just such large numbers.

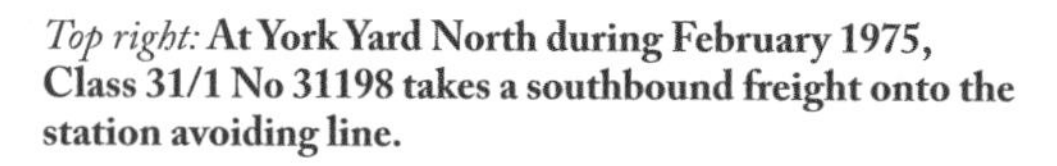

Top right: **At York Yard North during February 1975, Class 31/1 No 31198 takes a southbound freight onto the station avoiding line.**

Centre right: **Sister loco No 31275 approaches York from the north with a passenger train on 25 February 1979.**

Right: **Class 31/1 No 31294 passes York Yard North approaching the station with a parcels train during August 1979.**

Below: **The East Coast Main Line is the location once again as two Class 31/1s, led by No 31284, head north away from York on 6 May 1986.**

Nicknamed 'Tractors' as a result of the agricultural sound of their diesel engines, they became highly successful on both passenger and freight workings, with a total of 309 being built between 1960 and 1965 at the Vulcan Foundry and RSH works of English Electric. The locos were originally numbered D6700-D6999 and D6600-D6608, and in body design bore a strong family resemblance to other English Electrics such as the Class 40s and the Class 23 'Baby Deltics'. With

Above: **Class 37 No 37083 threads her train through York station on 21 February 1975.**

TOPS renumbering, the D6700 series became Nos 37001-37299, while at the same time the D6600 batch became Nos 37000–37308.

Equally at home on passenger and freight workings, the Class 37s became the standard Type 3 locos for BR, following the withdrawal of other Type 3 classes and many Type 2s in the 1980s. At that time the locos were given a major refurbishment and heavy overhaul, mainly at BREL Crewe, to prolong their life beyond the 1990s, and some were fitted with ETH. This work created a series of sub-classes, of which the 37/7s were arguably the most memorable, being modified to haul the heaviest freight workings such as were associated with the Llanwern, Port Talbot and Scunthorpe steel works.

Such has been the reliability of the class that as of 2011 some were still in main-line service despite being 50 years old, and demand

Above right: **On the East Coast Main Line north of York, Class 37 No 37082 runs south with a train load of new track.**

Right: **Captured at Pilmoor, Class 37 No 37152 races towards York with a passenger train from the north on 18 April 1979.**

At York Yard North on 8 July 1979 No 37096 waits to take her train northwards on the East Coast Main Line as preserved 'A4' No 4498 *Sir Nigel Gresley* prepares to reverse into the National Railway Museum.

certainly exists for their continued use on charter specials. In fact, West Coast Railways, well known as a steam rail tour operator with its headquarters at Carnforth, Lancashire, has four Class 37s running in service, Nos 37516, 37676, 37685 and 37706. In addition, well over 40 of the class have been purchased for preservation, including the first-built, No D6700, which is based at the National Railway Museum, York.

Other rescued 37s are located on heritage railways including the Mid Norfolk, North Norfolk, Eden Valley, East Lancashire, Gloucestershire Warwickshire, Severn Valley, Mid Hants, Bodmin & Wenford, Dean Forest, North Yorkshire Moors and Great Central. Further examples are in private ownership and undergoing restoration. In addition, a group called the Baby Deltic Project has procured No 37372 for conversion to a replica of a Class 23 'Baby Deltic'; this class of 10 English Electric Type 2s was built in 1959 but none survived. Fortunately, the Napier Deltic T9-29 engine (a half-size version of that used in the Class 55 'Deltics') and the generator from the last of the class to be cut up have survived and have been restored to operational condition at the Deltic

Above: **West Coast Railways' Class 37 No 37706, the only surviving Class 37/7 in the UK, hauls 'Black 5' No 44932 to Scarborough from York with the 'Scarborough Spa Express' on 9 August 2011. Having suffered a faulty injector prior to the first leg of the tour, from York to Wakefield and back (which was taken by the Class 37), the 'Black 5' was repaired at the NRM, but insufficient steam pressure could be achieved in time for the second leg to Scarborough. Later, No 44932 would haul the remainder of the tour with No 37706 returning light engine to York during the afternoon.**

Right: **The National Railway Museum's Class 37, class pioneer No D6700, outshopped in BR Green, is seen here working on the North Yorkshire Moors Railway at Grosmont, having brought in a train from Pickering on 11 May 2008 during the railway's 'Diesel Gala Weekend'. The NYMR is also home to sister loco No 37264.**

Preservation Society's MPD at Barrow Hill. No 37372 has been re-engined with the T9 engine and the loco body will be rebuilt and mounted on Class 20 bogies to create the replica.

In addition to those Class 37s that have found a new lease of life on our heritage railways, more than 40 are owned by Direct Rail Services and operate on the national network, being employed, for example, on engineering duties, track maintenance trains and special freight operations.

Right: **Direct Rail Services Class 37s Nos 37218 and 37608, based at the company's Carlisle Kingmoor depot, are parked in the station sidings at York on 31 January 2013 following their use on snow clearance duties.**

Below: **On an altogether more prestigious working, DRS Class 37s Nos 37609 and 37603 double-head 1Z 83, Compass Tours' 'The Pennine and North Eastern Explorer' from Milton Keynes to Durham and return. They are seen accelerating away from York on 24 July 2013.**

8. The purpose-built heavy freight locomotives

In an article for the January 1976 issue of *Railway World* entitled 'Diesel Electric Freight Locomotives for BR', it was reported that a wind of change appeared to be permeating the thinking on locomotive design, with the questioning of the 'mixed-traffic concept' and the suggestion by Mr G. S. W. Calder, Chief Mechanical & Electrical Engineer, BRB, that it was unlikely 'that locomotives would ever again be designed in an endeavour to meet both passenger and freight requirements'. At that time pressure was also growing to move long-distance freight back onto the railways to ease congestion on the increasingly overcrowded roads. Urgent reform of BR's dated freight network was urgently needed, including a radical rethink of the whole process of transporting goods, in order to establish an efficient and competitive alternative to the expanding motorway system.

At the forefront of this new thinking was the extension of TOPS (Total Operations Processing System) to encompass the freight sector. Introduced from 1973 for locomotive numbering, freight control by TOPS was completed on 27 October 1975, when Minister of Transport Dr John Gilbert formally switched on the computers and associated equipment in London that would handle information coming in from 152 Area Freight Centres at marshalling yards and principal freight depots throughout British Rail. TOPS would allow more efficient use of wagons by rapidly dispatching empty stock to an appropriate destination for immediate reuse. In the first year of operation, TOPS was predicted to save £3 million in reduced operating and maintenance costs, allowing 11,000 surplus wagons to be taken out of service, and it was expected to generate more revenue as it attracted increased business to the more efficient service.

The plan envisaged a new generation of heavy freight locos, able to move their trains at almost double the speeds previously achieved, with wagons of double the capacity. These express freights, travelling at near passenger train speeds, would operate on what is known as the Air-braked Freight Network, which was begun in 1972 with the Bristol-Glasgow route, followed a year later by the East Anglia-Scotland service. In October 1976 Railfreight added other express freight routes, including Dover-London-Warrington-Glasgow-Dundee, Birmingham-Sheffield-Leeds-York-Newcastle, and Humberside-Leeds-Carlisle-Glasgow. Plans were to create a full nationwide network delivering goods the same day or overnight between commercial centres.

By using TOPS to operate the system efficiently, the new range of wagons could be assembled into trains that could travel safely at up to 75mph, due to their air-operated disc brake system and High Speed Freight Vehicle suspensions. The initial success of the venture prompted further investment, and in 1977 the name 'Speedlink' was used for the first time in connection with the air-braked goods service. In 1983 Railfreight Distribution established the Speedlink Distribution Service – the final development of its air-braked 'wagon-load' service, based in 12 main marshalling yards at Glasgow (Mossend), Carlisle, Newcastle (Tyne), York (Dringhouses), Warrington, Leeds (Healey Mills), Doncaster, Toton, Whitemoor, Bescot (Birmingham), Willesden and Severn Tunnel Junction.

However, there were also a number of privately owned freight terminals, so competition was intense, so much so that Speedlink suffered heavy losses and the network was finally closed down in 1991. However, this was not the end of the air-braked freight service, as in 1994 Transrail (one of the three pre-privatisation train-load haulage companies) reintroduced the service under the working name 'Enterprise'. Later, the privatised freight train operator English, Welsh & Scottish Railway (EWS), having acquired five of the six freight companies created by the break-up of BR, developed the service further such that freight train movements increased by about 60% between 1994 and 1998. The acquisitions included Rail Express Systems in 1995, followed in 1996 by the three train-load companies from BR days – Loadhaul Ltd, Mainline Freight Ltd and Transrail Freight Ltd – then by Railfreight Distribution in 1997, leaving only Freightliner as a major competitor at the time. Nevertheless, in spite of major investment by EWS, including new locomotives and wagons, the predicted freight train speeds of 70mph-plus had not materialised by the late 1990s, with more than 90% of freight trains still being timed to run at 60mph or less.

In 2007 EWS was acquired by Deutsche Bahn AG, and in 2009 it adopted the DB Schenker brand. Meanwhile, the UK's second largest railfreight operator, Freightliner Group Ltd (previously part of British Rail, until privatised), was providing trunk rail services between key ports and inland railfreight interchanges, with Freightliner Heavy Haul operating nationwide in the bulk freight market for coal, aggregates, cement and petroleum products. In addition to these two major players, a third, GB Railfreight (GBRf), was founded in 1999 by GB Railways to operate various types of freight traffic including intermodal services, coal trains and chemical/petrochemical bulk transport. Having been acquired by First Group in 2003, it was later bought by Eurotunnel in May 2010.

These are the companies at the forefront of the revitalisation of UK freight on our railways, bringing massive investment in a new generation of locomotives and rolling stock, and fresh thinking to the question of how to attract freight customers back to the railways.

This new outlook was characterised by the realisation of a need for a fleet of purpose-built diesel freight locomotives, at the spearhead of which were a total of 135 Class 56 locos built between 1976 and 1984. Although the first 30 locomotives, Nos 56001-56030, built in Romania, were poorly constructed and withdrawn early, the remaining 105, built by BREL at Doncaster Works (Nos 56031-56115) and Crewe Works (Nos 56116-56135), proved to be strong and capable locomotives. For those of us brought up in the steam era of locomotive-hauled trains, the prospect of large, powerful diesels hauling freight, to supplement large, powerful diesels hauling express passenger trains, would go some way to easing the pain caused by the end of steam in 1968.

Hauling a heavy track train northwards along the ECML north of York near Shipton by Beningbrough on 9 July 1984 is a brace of Class 56s, Nos 56131 and 56126.

The Class 56 locos employed the air-brake system only (unlike previous designs that had vacuum brakes or a dual braking system fitted), and their more robust power units (using self-exciting alternators rather than DC generators) were a further advancement in design and therefore in performance. The fleet was operated mainly by EWS (having inherited it from its predecessors Transrail and Loadhaul in the 1990s), but availability and maintenance issues combined to render the locos less competitive in their later life, when more advanced types such as the Class 66 became available. Most were withdrawn by EWS in 2004 and, though many remained in store, new owner DB Schenker put them up for sale in 2011 and most went to scrap, with a few being sold on to private operators. According to the website of the Class 56 Group, seven of the class are preserved: No 56040 at Barrow Hill, withdrawn from service; 56086 and 56098 operating on the Battlefield Line; 56097 at the GCR's Nottingham Heritage Centre; 56101 working on the Mid Norfolk Railway; and two of the overhauled and reclassified locos, Nos 56301 (formerly 56045) and 56302 (56124) at Hitchin On Track Plant Depot, later moved to Barrow Hill Engine Shed in April 2011.

Later in the 1970s BR was keen to improve its stock of freight locomotives and also to enter the increasingly lucrative export market. With this in mind, the contract to build 50 Class 58 locos was awarded to BREL at Doncaster, and the new locos entered service in 1983. Though meant to be an improvement on the Class 56 in terms of performance and reduced maintenance costs, this turned out not to be the case, and problems with wheel-slip plagued their operation. Intended for use mainly on coal traffic, they were widely employed on general freight throughout the network, but their flaws, including the expense of maintenance, led to their removal from use (largely by

Above: **The former No 56057 *British Fuels* is now overhauled and refurbished as No 56311 and operated by British American Railway Services (of which DCR – Devon & Cornwall Railways – is an Open Access Operator). She is seen passing the site of Bolton Percy station, between York and Leeds, on hire to Colas Rail Freight, with train 6Z58, the Cheddleston to Stockton scrap metal working, on 4 December 2012.**

Below: **Sister loco No 56312 (formerly 56003) waits at Holgate Sidings with the same working on 28 March 2013. She now carries no branding, though she formerly carried advertising for Railfest 2012, which has since been removed.**

Right: **Now preserved as No 56301 by the Class 56 Group and housed at the Barrow Hill Roundhouse, the former No 56045 was overhauled and refurbished by Brush Traction. She is seen approaching York on the ECML near Colton Junction on 23 April 2013. *Rick Ward***

EWS) and their placement in long-term storage in 1999. Some were also exported to such countries as the Netherlands, Spain and France, though the French locos were returned to the UK in 2007, and placed back into storage.

At least one member of the class has been preserved. No 58016 was bought by the Class 58 Locomotive Group and is housed at Barrow Hill Roundhouse near Chesterfield, with sister loco No 58045 being under negotiation for purchase as a spares donor. Other stored members of the class have also been put up for sale by DB Schenker and at the time of writing were awaiting offers.

Above: **Class 58 No 58014 is seen at Toton, Nottinghamshire, during April 1988.** ***Rick Ward***

Below: **Class 59 No 59001** ***Yeoman Endeavour*** **is on display at Doncaster Works Open Day, in revised Foster Yeoman livery, on 27 July 2003.** ***Phil Scott***

Next into production came the Class 59 locos, built by General Motors Electro Motive Division between 1985 and 1995. Though only 15 were introduced, the Class 59s and their derivatives (sub-classes 59/1 and 59/2) are still successfully operated by DB Schenker and Mendip Rail, to haul heavy trains of coal, limestone and aggregates, with modifications allowing their maximum speed to be increased to 75mph.

Right: **EWS Class 60 No 60071 *Ribblehead Viaduct* passes the site of the former station at Bolton Percy, between Leeds and York, with train 4Z79, the Redcar to Dow Low stone hoppers, on 4 December 2012.**

The success of these locos led BR to place orders for a new high-powered Type 5 diesel for its Trainload Freight operations, created in 1988 to operate 'block train' schedules, where the whole train is composed of single-origin, single-commodity and single-destination stock. One hundred Class 60 locos were thus ordered, and though the privatisation of BR following the Railways Act of 1993 led to the splitting up of the trainload business, the individual companies formed later became part of the EWS consortium, then later again DB Schenker. Built between 1989 and 1993 by Brush Traction, the Class 60s replaced the Class 56 and Class 58 freight locos operating heavy stone, aggregates, ballast, steel

Above right: **The Class 60 Preservation Group was formed in 2008 with a view to preserving at least one member of the class. Since 2009 many Class 60s have been in storage, with only about 15 being operational at any one time, though DB Schenker indicated that it planned to overhaul several of its stored fleet at some future date. True to its word, by 2011-12 around 20 of the company's fleet of Class 60s were scheduled to receive a heavy overhaul and be returned to front-line service. One such is No 60010, seen here passing Shipton by Beningbrough on the ECML north of York with a heavy freight train on 8 November 2012.**

Right: **DB Schenker Class 60 No 60020 hauls a train of steel girders north towards York along the ECML at Colton Junction on 9 April 2013.**

Resplendent in the early spring sunshine, DB Schenker's Class 66 No 66097 passes Bolton Percy heading towards York with a train of coal empties on 14 March 2013. ***Rick Ward***

and petroleum trains.

And so to the 'Sheds' – the EMD Class 66. Most of BR's freight operations had been bought by EWS following privatisation, but many of the locomotives were nearing the end of their useful lives, or were of doubtful reliability, so EWS approached General Motors Electro Motive Division (EMD) with a view to buying in a replacement fleet. What was offered was that company's JT42CWR, a development of its successful Class 59 design, with important modifications and improvements. Initially classified as Class 61, the new locos were redesignated Class 66 in the TOPS system, and 250 were ordered and built in Canada. Soon afterwards, further orders for the design were placed by Freightliner, GB Railfreight and Direct Rail Services, bringing the total number built between 1998 and 2008 to 446.

In the York area the Class 66 locos are the most frequently encountered traction seen at the head of the numerous freight services that daily pass through the city, being especially well represented on the coal trains feeding the nearby ever-hungry power stations of Drax, Eggborough and Ferrybridge.

Nicknamed 'Sheds' by enthusiasts, due to their front-end appearance, they displaced several of their predecessors, including the Class 47s and 57s, as well as the earlier 'purpose-built' freight locos, as a consequence of their high

Centre: **Heading north on the ECML at Colton Junction on 6 May 2011, Class 66/0 No 66094 heads an EWS freight.**

Above: **Class 66/7 No 66727 takes a GBRf train north towards the junction and York from the Sherburn-in-Elmet direction on 22 July 2011.**

Left: **In GBRf blue livery, Class 66/7 No 66725 passes Colton Junction, York, on 9 September 2011.**

Centre: **Sister loco No 66721 heads in the opposite direction towards York and the north on 29 November 2011, sporting the livery of Metronet Rail. Metronet Rail was one of two companies in a public-private partnership with London Underground, the other being Tube Lines Ltd. It was responsible for the maintenance of nine London Underground lines; however, it suffered a severe financial crisis and went into administration in 2007, ceasing to exist in 2011 when the formal process of liquidation was completed.**

Below: **In Direct Rail Services livery, Class 66/4 No 66431 heads an intermodal train south towards York on the ECML neat Shipton by Beningborough on 18 May 2012. The 15 locos operated by DRS (Nos 66420-66434) were intended for use on such intermodal traffic but the company, having been formed by British Nuclear Fuels Ltd in 1995, also operates all nuclear flask trains in Britain, which were previously the responsibility of EWS, and before that British Rail. Though the Class 66s are used for this traffic, they are considered to be overpowered for such work.**

reliability and superior performance. Many are in service on intermodal traffic, being operated by DB Schenker, Freightliner, GBRf Europorte, Direct Rail Services and Colas Rail, and run to the maximum freight speed of 75mph.

Such has been the success of the design that EMD now markets the loco throughout Europe under its well-known British identity as 'Series 66'. Members of the class can be seen operating in Germany, the Netherlands, Belgium, Luxemburg, Sweden, Norway, Denmark, France and Poland, as well as on international routes between these countries. They are also currently operated by Egyptian National Railways.

The huge success of the Class 66 locos throughout Europe and beyond might give the impression that they have been problem free and popular with all concerned in their operation. However, the one flaw in their

Above right: **GBRf operates the 46 locos of Class 66/7 on coal and intermodal services. Though since 2010 owned by Europorte, a subsidiary of Eurotunnel, the company has reverted to using the original name of GB Railfreight. Following the recent very welcome trend, most of the locos in the class have been named. Here No 66707 *Sir Sam Fay* heads north away from York on the ECML near Shipton by Beningbrough with a train of coal empties on 10 March 2012.**

Right: **No 66708 *Jayne* is a little further north passing Railway Cottages Crossing on 16 May 2012.**

Below: **Two days after the previous picture, No 66717 *Good Old Boy* is seen being passed by a Virgin IC125 Cross Country set as they too head north from York.**

design seems to be in the area of driver comfort, especially in relation to noise levels, vibration and excessive temperatures in the cab in hot weather. Serious complaints from drivers both in the UK and in mainland Europe led to the threat of industrial action (in the UK) and to increased pay for drivers of this type of locomotive (in Norway). Improvements in noise reduction and cooling systems have been introduced on some UK locomotives to create a more acceptable working environment for drivers.

Top left: **One of the few as yet unnamed class members, No 66743, hauls a loaded coal train towards the power stations south of York on 18 May 2012.**

Top right: **Colas Rail Freight Class 66/8 No 66848 heads its train of loaded coal hoppers south along the ECML near Shipton by Beningbrough, north of York, on 1 November 2012. The Colas Group is a company based mainly in France, but with subsidiaries in the UK and Belgium, providing materials and services for the transport industry, including road and rail. Colas Rail is heavily involved in the maintenance and upgrading of the UK rail network, having become the country's largest contractor specialising in high-output track renewal. The company is also an important provider for projects including electrification and freight handling, using a fleet of Class 47, 56 and 66 locos and on-track plant.**

Above left: **No 66848 is seen in action again on 15 November 2012 passing Colton Junction and heading west from York.**

Above: **Waiting at Holgate sidings on 16 April 2013 is Colas Class 66 No 66849 *Wylam Dilly*, with a train of empty coal hoppers. The original 'Wylam Dilly' was sister locomotive to the better-known 'Puffing Billy', and was built by William Hedley in 1813 for use at Wylam Colliery near Newcastle-upon-Tyne. The pair represent the oldest surviving locomotives in the world and were withdrawn from service in 1862. 'Wylam Dilly' is now on display at the Royal Scottish Museum in Edinburgh.**

Top: **Class 66 No 66414 hurries south along the ECML through Colton Junction on 3 April 2013, resplendent in Freightliner Blue (Tesco) livery.**

Centre left **On the same day as the previous picture, No 66956 takes a loaded coal train west away from York, carrying the familiar Freightliner green and yellow colours.**

Centre right: **GBRf's No 66720 carries an unusual Class 66 livery, painted with a design entitled 'night and day', being a colour scheme devised by a young schoolgirl for a competition. The loco is seen here heading west away from York past Colton with a loaded coal train on 3 February 2012.**

Above: **On one of the more unusual Class 66 workings seen recently in the York area was GBRf's Nos 66723 *Chinook* and 66727 *Andrew Scott CBE* passing Colton 'top-and-tailing' a Rail Head Treatment Train heading for York on 14 November 2012. *Rick Ward***

Finally with regard to this highly successful design, and emphasising its international credentials, GBRf has recently acquired three former Dutch Class 66s, Nos 66747, 66748 and 66749, which can regularly be seen hauling trains in the York area.

One of the latest additions to the express freight category of diesel locomotives has been the Class 67, introduced to be operated by EWS for the specific purpose of hauling high-speed mail trains across the whole network. Thirty locos were built in Valencia, Spain, by Alstom between 1999 and 2000, but in 2003 the EWS/Royal Mail contract was terminated, so these new locos, designed for a top speed of 125mph, had to be found employment elsewhere. Their ability to supply train heating and air conditioning made them suitable for express passenger duties, and in particular they found a role heading luxury trains such as the 'Northern Belle' and the 'Venice-Simplon Orient Express', as well as other charters, replacing the once ubiquitous Class 47s.

Nicknamed 'Skips' by railway enthusiasts as a result of their less than aesthetically pleasing appearance, they have nonetheless filled a gap in the market, and have also

Top: **Former Dutch Railways' No 66749 in GBRf grey livery approaches York through Colton Junction with train 6H30, composed of new Drax coal hoppers.**

Above: **Sister loco No 66747 is seen double-heading a heavy coal train bound for Drax Power Station, with the contrasting livery of No 66720, also passing Colton Junction.**

Above: **On the ECML north of York, Class 67 No 67001, with No 67030 at the rear, brings Day 4 of 'The Arran & West Highlander' rail tour south from Edinburgh to King's Cross on 13 April 2009.**

Left: **'Thunderbirds are Go!' EWS Class 67 No 67024 from Doncaster speeds away from York towards Darlington, light engine, on Saturday 8 June 2013 on a mission to rescue No 91112 and its train (1E04, the 06.55 Edinburgh to King's Cross service), which had failed there with an electrical fire in the loco. It was expected that the 'Thunderbird' would later drag the failed set to Bounds Green HST & Electric Loco Service Depot near London.**

found employment in such diverse roles as on the 'Caledonian Sleeper' trains operated by First ScotRail and as 'Thunderbird' rescue locomotives for failed trains on the ECML (see below). The locos were originally painted in EWS maroon livery, but in more recent times have been seen in a variety of colour schemes. Most notable among these occurred in 2003 when Nos 67005 and 67006 replaced the previous Class 47s hauling the Royal Train, and were thus painted in Royal Claret and named *Queen's Messenger* and *Royal Sovereign*.

The purpose-built freight diesels have earned themselves almost 'cult status' in the eyes of railway enthusiasts, seldom failing to impress as they heave their heavy goods trains up and down the network, with lots of engine noise and exhaust 'clag'. Sporting the liveries of the various train operating companies adds another dimension to their attraction, and as the lobby to move more heavy freight by rail rather than road continues to gain support, we can look forward to the introduction of the next generation of specialist diesel locos such as the 30 Class 70 units, under construction since 2008 by General Electric in Erie, Pennsylvania, and currently being delivered to the UK for use by Freightliner UK, and the 15 Class 68s ordered by Direct Rail Services from Vossloh in Spain, and planned for delivery in 2014.

9. Electrics to Scotland

The electrification of the ECML was not begun until 1985 and was completed by late 1990, at which time the 'Inter City 225s' were introduced. These trains consist of a Class 91 electric locomotive hauling nine Mark 4 coaches and a Driving Van Trailer (DVT), which is a Control Car resembling the locomotive, allowing the driver to operate the loco from the opposite end of the train. The 31 Class 91 hauled sets were a spin-off from the Advanced Passenger Train project, which was abandoned in the 1980s; the locos were built by BREL at Crewe Works and the coaching stock at GEC-Alstom in Birmingham. Originally classified as Class 91/0 and numbered 91001 to 91031, they were later (2000-02) refurbished by Adtranz/Bombardier at Doncaster, reclassified under TOPS to Class 91/1 and renumbered 91101 to 91122 and 91124 to 91132 (loco number 91023 was unlucky enough to have been involved in both the Hatfield rail crash and the Great Heck rail crash, so after refurbishment in 2001 it was renumbered 91132 rather than 91123, perhaps to encourage a change of fortune). The DVTs are numbered 82101-82152, 82200-82231 and 82301-82308.

Operating over the ECML and the Glasgow to Carstairs section of the WCML, the InterCity 225s, though generating a massive 6,300hp, are restricted to a top speed of 125mph. Due to the lack of in-cab signalling on the British railway system (except for High Speed One – the Channel Tunnel link), which warns drivers of possible hazards on the route ahead, all trains are limited to this speed to guarantee a safe stopping distance between signals in case of emergency.

Since the privatisation of BR, the IC 225s are owned by Eversholt Rail Group (formerly HSBC Rail UK Ltd), one of three major Rolling Stock Operating Companies in the UK, owning around one-third of the passenger locomotives, multiple units and coaching stock running on Network Rail's system, which it leases to various train operators such as East Coast and GNER.

Top: **Sporting its original InterCity livery, power car No 91014 is at the rear of an Edinburgh to King's Cross service as it enters York station on 18 July 1994.**

Above: **DVT No 82200 leads an East Coast set towards York with an Edinburgh to King's Cross express near Shipton by Beningbrough on 13 April 2009.**

Top: Racing south towards London King's Cross in the freezing conditions of winter 2010, Class 91/1 No 91130 is at the rear of the train as it passes Colton Junction, York, on 3 December.

Above left: Heading for York on the ECML on 18 May 2012 is an IC 225 set headed by DVT No 82231, looking smart in its livery of GNER blue with East Coast white stripe.

Above right: Class 225 power car No 91117 *West Riding Limited*, sporting East Coast silver livery, leads her set into York station past Holgate, recalling the heyday of steam when the King's Cross to Leeds and Bradford service regularly featured one of Sir Nigel Gresley's iconic 'A4' 'Pacifics'.

Left: The outside observation gallery at the National Railway Museum in York affords excellent views of the trains passing through the impressive station, such as this East Coast IC 225 set led by No 91122, seen leaving with the 14.32 service to Glasgow Central via Edinburgh on 8 November 2012.

Above: **Still regarded by many as the ECML's 'flagship' service, the 'Flying Scotsman' continues to hurry between London King's Cross and Edinburgh on a daily basis, having been resurrected into the East Coast timetable from the summer of 2011. Carrying East Coast Railway's distinctive 'Flying Scotsman' livery, Class 91 No 91101 races through Colton Junction, York, on 15 November 2012 with the northbound service from King's Cross.**

Left: **The same loco waits at York station to take the return service to London King's Cross on 7 February 2013.**

Left: **Heading south from York through Colton Junction on 30 March 2013 is IC 225 No 91110 *Battle of Britain Memorial Flight*, named during the Railfest 2012 event at the NRM, York, which featured a Lancaster, Hurricane and Spitfire 'flypast'. No 91110 holds the UK speed record for electric traction of 162mph, set on Stoke Bank on 17 September 1989. *Rick Ward***

Completing the current tally of special liveries, No 91007 carries the James Bond 'Skyfall' promotion with a King's Cross to York service passing Colton Junction on 19 February 2013.

No 91007 leaves York station for King's Cross on 28 March 2013.

The British Rail Class 90 electric locos were built by BREL at Crewe between 1987 and 1990. Fifty units were produced, Nos 90001-90050, designed to haul express passenger and heavy freight trains and to replace the aging fleet of Class 81 to 85 electric locos dating back to the 1960s. In the early 1990s 26 of the locos were designated for freight traffic, reclassified as Class 90/1, renumbered 90125-90150 and restricted to a maximum speed of 75mph (from their original designated 110mph). A further five of the class were dedicated to postal trains. Nos 90016-90020 worked as such on Euston-Glasgow, King's Cross-Newcastle and Birmingham-Glasgow services. Upon the privatisation of BR in 1996, the fleet was divided between several operators including DB Schenker, Freightliner, Greater Anglia (formerly National Express East Anglia) and Virgin Trains.

A King's Cross to Newcastle postal service arrives at York in Rail Express Systems livery on 29 May 2003, with Class 90 No 90017 in charge. This loco was one of five acquired from Rail Express Systems and operated by DB Schenker, until being put up for sale in 2011.

Leading a northbound Royal Mail postal service from King's Cross to York on 30 March 2013 is EWS Class 90 No 90039. *Rick Ward*

10. Yet steam lives on...

Crowds of enthusiasts flock to York station on Saturday 5 July 2008 to witness Gresley 'A4' 'Pacific' No 60009 *Union of South Africa* leaving for Edinburgh Waverley with the second stage of 'The Coronation' rail tour. Organised by the Steam Dreams rail charter company to celebrate the 70th anniversary of *Mallard*'s run of 3 July 1938, when the 'A4' set the world speed record for steam of 126mph – still the fastest achieved by any steam locomotive – No 60009 had taken over from sister loco No 60007 *Sir Nigel Gresley*, which had brought in the first stage from King's Cross. Next day saw the return journey hauled by No 60009 from Edinburgh to York, with the final stage back to King's Cross in the care of a third 'A4', No 60019 *Bittern*, a total of almost 800 miles behind the 'A4s'.

For myself and many fellow enthusiasts the atmosphere of depression that followed the end of steam in 1968 has been lifted in the sense that we have come to terms with the new era – an era in which powerful diesels and hill-flattening electrics have kept our interest alive. More than that, it has given us something else to enthuse about. The 'corporate image' of BR has gone. Privatisation has generated not only massive and much-needed investment in locomotives and rolling stock, but also to some degree has resulted in a return to the individuality and competitiveness that was such a powerful driving force at the height of the Steam Age. And while all this has been going on, the fire has been rekindled. The steam preservation movement, once given up for dead by so many, has emerged like a phoenix from the ashes, to become a major player in its own right. More than 60 standard-gauge heritage railways prosper in every region of the UK, providing a home for more than 300 main-line diesel locomotives in addition to their steam fleets, and special charter excursions form an almost everyday feature on our rail network. On the internet, specialist websites and rail groups keep us informed and allow sharing of news and views about all the current and planned tours and loco movements.

Steam-hauled rail tours, though now fewer in total than at their height a decade ago, still number in the region of more than 250 trains annually, featuring locomotives drawn from a pool of almost 50 that have current main-line running certificates, or are expected to receive certification in the coming months, and which still proudly represent the former GWR, SR, LNER and LMS of the 'glory years'. All in all, it is a healthy variety to keep us coming back for more. And we do, in droves, young and old, male and female, families with small children, all drawn by the spell of steam and the inexplicable attraction that is the railway track.

Above: **A quartet of 'A4s' at York for a unique photo call: left to right, Nos 60009 *Union of South Africa*, 60007 *Sir Nigel Gresley*, 60019 *Bittern* and 4468 *Mallard*. York's local newspaper, *The Press*, ran the headline 'Four Giants of Steam Together Again' above a photo of the crowd gathered outside the NRM in the pouring rain. The caption read, 'Rail enthusiasts were treated to one of the most spectacular sights in the history of steam locomotive preservation in York this weekend ... [when] the National Railway Museum reunited four magnificent A4 steam locomotives for the first time since their hey-day.' It went on, 'There are only six A4 locomotives remaining in the world – four in the UK, one in the USA and one in Canada.' Perhaps prophetically, an article by David Wilcock had appeared in the April/May 2008 issue of *Heritage Railway* magazine urging the repatriation of the two 'A4s' currently languishing in exile in North America. In his article under the title 'Okay you guys, its time you gave us back our A4 Pacifics', Mr Wilcock questioned the reasoning behind their export more than 40 years ago and put the case most vigorously for their return 'to the country of their creation, where they will be respected.' *Peter Webb***

The popularity of steam locos today is taken for granted, and steam specials are enjoyed by a vast audience wherever they run, but this availability was hard won, for in the early days the management at BR were, if not openly hostile, certainly less than enthusiastic about the return of steam to our railways, and a total ban on steam-hauled trains was enforced after 1968.

The first preserved standard-gauge steam-operated passenger railway in the world had run its first train on 7 August 1960. The Bluebell Railway had opened its doors just three years after BR had closed the line from East Grinstead in West Sussex to Lewes in East Sussex, a distance of some 9 miles. Now, more than 50 years later, it boasts the largest collection of steam locomotives (more than 30) in the UK after the National Railway Museum, together with a stock of almost 150 carriages and wagons. Encouraged by its success, the ensuing years saw similar ventures springing up throughout the country, with some of the best-known pioneers being the Keighley & Worth Valley Railway (reopened in 1968), the Severn Valley and Great Central railways (1970), the East Somerset, Lakeside & Haverthwaite and North Yorkshire Moors railways (1973); the Kent & East Sussex Railway (1974); the West Somerset Railway (1976); and the Mid Hants 'Watercress Line' and Nene Valley railways (1977).

According to the Heritage Railway Association, which claims to be 'the voice of the heritage railway movement' in the UK, these are now among more than 170 heritage railways, railway centres, museums and cliff railways represented by that body – a far cry from those dark days of the late 1960s.

Preservation: the formative years, 1970s and 1980s

Though we often think of the two decades that followed the official 'end of steam on BR' as the time when railway preservation was born, in fact the railway preservation movement is a lot older than most people realise. It dates back to 1927, when a group of enthusiasts who had come together in Croydon in 1909, calling themselves the Stephenson Locomotive Society, bought the recently withdrawn LB&SCR 0-4-2 locomotive No 214 *Gladstone*, the first member of the 'B1' Class of 36 locos introduced in 1882. The decision to save *Gladstone* was a landmark for railway

Beside the turntable in the Great Hall of the National Railway Museum in York during May 1984 is the pioneering LB&SCR 0-4-2 No 214 *Gladstone*. Beyond her is a preserved 'Royal Saloon' teak coach used by Her Majesty Queen Victoria, and Gresley 'V2' 2-6-2 No 4771 *Green Arrow*, very much the youngster of the group, having been introduced only in 1936.

preservation as it marked the start of a process that escalated through the ensuing years, culminating in the extensive movement we enjoy today. This includes the National Collection of locos that, together with the pioneering *Gladstone*, adorn the worldwide magnet that is the National Railway Museum in York.

Among other projects predating the end of steam was one born in 1966 to save a single locomotive, but which blossomed to become one of the most successful railway centres in the country at the time. In that year the Bahamas (Stockport) Locomotive Society was formed with the aim of saving ex-LMS 'Jubilee' No 5596 *Bahamas* from the scrapyard. The loco was purchased for its scrap value of £3,000, followed a couple of years later by the purchase of a redundant and derelict depot with a single-road shed. Thus was born the Dinting Railway Centre and Museum, 1½ miles north-west of Glossop in Derbyshire, which at its peak boasted visits by such high-profile locos as *Flying Scotsman*, *Mallard* and the 'A2' *Blue Peter*, as well as various members of the LMS

Appropriately, No 214 *Gladstone* is displayed at the NRM York complete with the Royal Train decorations she carried for the Diamond Jubilee of Queen Victoria in 1897, seen here during 2009. She was transferred here as part of the National Collection when the museum opened in 1975, having been previously housed in York's 'old' Railway Museum in Queen Street since 1927. Between her wheel arches she carries the Royal coat of arms of the United Kingdom above a Royal Cipher.

'Jubilee' Class. However, as a result of a dispute over the ownership of the land, the site was abandoned in 1991, with the society and its collection moving to its new home at Ingrow West station near Keighley, West Yorkshire, on the Keighley & Worth Valley Railway.

The early 1970s had seen a begrudging acceptance by the railway management of the appeal of steam to the general public, following the success of the 'Bulmer's Cider Trains' in 1971, which persuaded BR to open a limited route mileage for steam haulage. The response was immediate and the public clamoured for more. BR management was forced to admit its initial error in banning steam, and the floodgates were gradually opened. York was ideally positioned to welcome this new Steam Age and did so with open arms. Steam-hauled excursions began to arrive on a regular basis, bringing enthusiasts from far and wide to enjoy the many and varied attractions offered by this historic city.

By the late 1970s the return of steam-hauled specials over Britain's main lines was being hailed as a major success story, including as it did the long-awaited decision to make the Settle and Carlisle route available for such trains. In an article for the January 1979 issue of *Railway World* magazine, Bernard Staite, Secretary of the Steam Locomotive Operators' Association, welcomed the intention of BR to operate its own main-line steam trips in the form of the 'Cumbrian Coast Express' based out of 'Steamtown', Carnforth, and the 'Yorkshire Circular', centred

Above right: **'B1' No 1306 *Mayflower* receives attention before continuing north from York with 'The North Eastern' rail tour of 21 September 1975.**

Right: **'A4' 'Pacific' No 4498 *Sir Nigel Gresley* arrives at York with an enthusiasts' charter on 7 September 1975.**

For a time the only steam loco granted permission to run over BR metals after the 'end of steam', ex-LNER 'A3' No 4472 *Flying Scotsman* arrives at York on 28 September 1975, re-enacting the legendary King's Cross to Edinburgh service.

on York and later to be re-routed and renamed the 'Scarborough Spa Express'. Signalling as these did a commitment to continue steam haulage over BR metals well into the 1980s, this, combined with BR's agreement that in future 'timing sheets' could be made available (albeit at a cost of £1 each plus a stamped addressed envelope!), and the inclusion of 'photographic stops' at interesting locations, all boded well for a future when steam would be welcome on our lines once more.

By 1980 36 steam locos had been certified for operating on BR, with more than 1,000 miles of lines approved for such running. The March 1980 issue of *The Railway Magazine*, in an article entitled 'BR Steam', gave details and noted that, in addition to this, a further

'The last one': BR 9F 2-10-0 No 92220 *Evening Star* prepares to take 'The Pioneer Express' away from York on 22 August 1976.

Left: **'V2' No 4771 *Green Arrow* races through Marston Moor station, on the approach to York from Harrogate, with the 'Yorkshire Circular' tour on 25 June 1978. This popular tour by way of Leeds and Harrogate paved the way for the 'Scarborough Spa Express', one of Yorkshire's steam 'success stories'.**

Below: **Preserved LMS 'Jubilee' No 5690 *Leander* is seen at speed near Bolton Percy heading for York with the Dinting Railway Centre tour 'The Mancunian' on 28 October 1978.**

19 steam locos had been approved to run with temporary certificates to allow their inclusion in the 'Rocket 150' celebrations of 24-26 May, at which time routes into Manchester Victoria from Liverpool Edge Hill, Hellifield via Blackburn, and Guide Bridge would also be used for steam haulage as part of the programme for the re-enactment of the 'Rainhill Trials' of October 1829.

Among the locos parading at the re-enactment were replicas of three of the five entries that took part in the original competition, *Rocket*, *Novelty* and *Sans Pareil*. As only *Rocket* completed the trials, its designers and builders George and Robert Stephenson were awarded the contract to build locomotives for the newly opened Liverpool & Manchester Railway. Other notable steam locos at 'Rocket

Left: **Following an afternoon in the city, *Leander* was piloted home by Midland 'Compound' No 1000, the pair are seen steaming through Copmanthorpe.**

Below: **Resplendent in Apple Green livery, 'V2' No 4771 *Green Arrow* is seen again entering York at the head of 'The Northumbrian Limited' on 7 April 1979.**

150' included *Lion*, at the time the oldest operable steam locomotive in existence; the LNER trio of No 4472 *Flying Scotsman*, 'V2' No 4771 *Green Arrow* and No 4498 *Sir Nigel Gresley*; LMS 'Jubilee' No 5690 *Leander*, No 6201 *Princess Elizabeth* and 'Coronation' Class No 46229 *Duchess of Hamilton*; GWR 0-6-0 No 3205 and 'Castle' Class No 5051 *Drysllwyn Castle*; SR Bulleid 'Merchant Navy' Class No 35028 *Clan Line*; Midland Railway 'Compound' No 1000; LNWR 2-4-0 No 790 *Hardwicke*; and BR's 'last build', 9F No 92220 *Evening Star*. These were accompanied by a host of other steam, diesel and electric locomotives representing the development of traction since those pioneering days.

Even by the early 1980s questions were still being asked about the viability of preserved steam locomotives. In an article for the May 1981 edition of *Steam Railway* magazine entitled 'Can Preservation Survive?', Michael Draper, General Manager of the Severn Valley Railway, considered that 'there is a limited market and a surfeit of steam'. Conceding that preserved railways were generally doing 'a good job', he bemoaned the fact that most were nowhere near forward-thinking enough. He advocated the policy of loco exchanges

Top: **'A3' No 4472** ***Flying Scotsman*** **is seen at York MPD after having been in charge of the 'Yorkshire Circular' of 27 May 1979.**

Centre: **At Poppleton station, between York and Harrogate, LNER 'V2' No 4771** ***Green Arrow*** **brings the 'Yorkshire Circular' back to York during August 1979.**

Left: **Passing Long Marston station on the same route, also during August 1979, LNER 'A3' No 4472** ***Flying Scotsman*** **is at the head of the 'Yorkshire Circular' rail tour.**

A welcome visitor from the 'Southern', between duties at York MPD during August 1979, is Bulleid 'Merchant Navy' 'Pacific' No 35028 *Clan Line*.

and main-line preparation of locos using in-house engineering facilities, noting that 'better standards bring prestige and publicity, and are good for morale.' He went on to conclude that 'the best standard must be the main-line certificate standard, so this is the least we should impose on our own railway.'

By the mid-1980s BR's 'Scarborough Spa Express' from York was being acknowledged as a great success, while operations based on 'Steamtown', Carnforth, had expanded to include the provision of major restoration and mechanical overhaul facilities, put to good use on projects such as the refurbishment of Pullman coach sets for the 'Northern Belle' and 'Cumbrian Mountain Pullman' rail tours, this work being in addition to its function as an important working steam centre.

Bringing 'The Comet' rail tour into York past Dringhouses on 29 September 1979 is Gresley 'A4' No 4498 *Sir Nigel Gresley*.

Left: **Stanier LMS 'Coronation' 'Pacific' No 46229 *Duchess of Hamilton* is always a welcome sight in York, and here she is seen waiting in Holgate Sidings before taking 'The White Rose' back to Carnforth on 4 August 1982.**

Below: **On a rainy 16 August 1983 'The Duchess' is in charge of the 'Scarborough Spa Express' heading for the coast near Bootham level crossing on the outskirts of York.**

Right: **The following pictures show some of the star performers on the 'Scarborough Spa Express' during the 1980s. In the first, 9F No 92220 *Evening Star* thunders away from Cross Gates on 14 August 1883. *Douglas Todd***

Above left: **'West Country' Class No 34092 *City of Wells* storms out of York on 30 July 1985. *Douglas Todd***

Above right: **LNER 'V2' No 4771 *Green Arrow* passes Burton Lane signal box heading for Scarborough during August 1986. *Douglas Todd***

Left: **'A4' No 4498 *Sir Nigel Gresley* is seen near Cross Gates on 15 August 1981. *Douglas Todd***

Below: **Passengers at York station were treated to the sight of the famous LNER 'A3' No 4472 *Flying Scotsman* on 25 May 1981. *Douglas Todd***

Above: **Perhaps even more impressive was the combined effect of Southern favourites No 34092 *City of Wells* and 'N15' Class No 777 *Sir Lamiel*, filling the station with steam on 13 August 1985.** ***Douglas Todd***

Left: **Gresley 'A4' No 4468 *Mallard* is back in steam again and on the East Coast Main Line at York station heading 'Mallard 88' on 17 July 1988. She is about to set off for Carlisle over the always challenging Settle and Carlisle route.**

Preservation comes of age: the 1990s

The early 1990s saw enormous growth within the railway preservation movement, with the demanding task of rescuing derelict locomotives from the vast scrapyard of Woodham Brothers at Barry continuing apace. Heritage railways throughout the land were attracting visitors in increasing numbers. As the memory of working steam faded, the nostalgia industry boomed, and nowhere more so than in York and its surroundings, for in addition to the excellent and thriving magnet of the National Railway Museum, the locality boasted three preserved lines. Near Skipton is the Yorkshire Dales Railway Trust, better known as the Embsay & Bolton Abbey Railway, based on the village of Embsay but with bold plans to expand to cater for the visitors to nearby Bolton Abbey as well as to the bustling market town of Skipton itself. With the glorious Yorkshire Dales on its doorstep, the railway is well placed to attract steam lovers from far and wide.

Also within easy travelling distance of York is the Keighley & Worth Valley Railway, whose complete branch line, restored to its original form, runs on steep gradients through the industrial landscape of the old West Riding to the moorland towns of Haworth and Oxenhope at the head of the valley. To the north of York, within the imposing scenery of the National Park, is the North Yorkshire Moors Railway, whose 18 miles boast a testing 1 in 49 climb out of Grosmont before traversing the top of the moors to Pickering. Connections to the coast at Whitby add to the attraction.

Steam loco preservation has always grabbed the attention of the public, and in the 1990s there were generous donations to the many 'appeals', but alongside this was a massive increase in the rush to purchase and restore diesel and electric locos that were constantly becoming 'life-expired' or simply 'surplus to requirements'. Among these the Class 08 and Class 20 diesels were particularly popular with potential buyers from the heritage railways. Perhaps more surprising was the surge in interest shown in traditional diesel multiple units (DMUs), now often referred to as 'first-generation' or 'heritage' units. As the number of examples declined on the network, the number being purchased for preservation soared, with more than 100 in the hands of preservationists by 1993, and many more in the process of being acquired. More recently, examples of the BREL-Leyland Class 141 'Pacer' DMUs have found a new lease of life on heritage railways. Twenty of these two-car sets were built from 1984 and worked mainly around the Leeds area of West Yorkshire until they were withdrawn in 1997, after which most were exported to work for the Islamic Republic of Iran Railways. Three units are operational in preservation, however, including No 141103, which can be found working on the Weardale Railway. The other remaining sets are owned by the Colne Valley Railway and the

Storming out of Grosmont station to attack the stiff climb ahead is former 'WD' 2-10-0 No 3672 *Dame Vera Lynn*, with one of the last steam-hauled services of the season for Pickering on 4 November 1990.

'Pacer' DMU set No 141103 pauses at Knaresborough on the Harrogate to York line during April 1991. Now preserved, it operates on the Weardale Railway near Bishop Auckland in County Durham.

Llangollen Railway.

But in many people's opinion, the preservation success story of the 1990s was undoubtedly that of steam. Preserved steam railways, and more especially steam on the main line, was what the public wanted to see, and the time was ripe to give the public what they wanted.

A consequence of the privatisation of the rail network following the Railways Act of 1993 was the establishment of Train Operating Companies (TOCs). These included more than 20 passenger TOCs, eight Freight Operating Companies and a number of Private Train Operators, such as the heritage railways. Those concerned with steam rail tours, such as West Coast Railways (WCR) and DB Schenker (in association with Riviera Trains), provide services through a system of tour promoters. WCR has been operating charter trains since 1998, both in its own right and on behalf of tour promoters including Compass Tours, The Railway Touring Company, The Scottish Railway Preservation Society (SRPS), Spitfire Railtours and Steam Dreams. It runs the 'Jacobite' steam train in the Scottish Highlands from its base at Fort William, the 'Cambrian' in North Wales and the 'Scarborough Spa Express' in Yorkshire from its main base and HQ at Carnforth, Lancashire, and has a depot at the former GWR site at Southall, West London, where much of its diesel fleet is housed.

DB Schenker also operates through Compass Tours, the SRPS and Steam Dreams, as well as with Pathfinder Tours and UK Railtours. Other companies promoting steam rail tours include Great Railway Journeys of Britain, the trading name of the South Coast Railway Company; the North Eastern Locomotive Preservation Group (NELPG), which has a base at Grosmont on the North Yorkshire Moors Railway; the National Railway Museum; Statesman Rail, operating Great British Railway Journeys, which includes 'The Fellsman' train over the Settle and Carlisle line; the 'Venice-Simplon Orient Express' (VSOE), which also operates 'The British Pullman', 'Northern Belle' and 'Royal Scotsman' luxury trains; and Vintage Trains Ltd, a subsidiary of the Birmingham Railway Museum Trust at Tyseley.

As a result of the activities of these and other rail tour promoters, enthusiasts have been able to indulge themselves on a diet of steam in a wide range of localities and featuring an impressive array of our finest preserved locos. For myself, lucky enough to live in the historic City of York, with all its railway connections, the opportunities are immense. In addition to the superb National Railway Museum, we have the regular summer steam services such as the 'Scarborough Spa Express' and the 'Scarborough Flyer', the numerous special excursions visiting or passing through the city, the mighty Settle and Carlisle line not far away, and several heritage lines within easy travelling distance. Thanks to the 'digital revolution' in photography, chasing trains is not the prohibitively expensive activity it might have been if we were still reliant on the developing and printing of film, though some of the artistic or creative element, derived from hours in the darkroom, has been lost. Some say 'no bad thing', but I'm not so sure…

11. York on show at the National Railway Museum

In 2000 the National Railway Museum (NRM), occupying the site of York North locomotive depot, celebrated the 25th anniversary of its opening on 26 September 1975 by HRH the Duke of Edinburgh. The following year the NRM won the 'European Museum of the Year' award, and plans were already afoot to create an 'extension' in County Durham. These plans came to fruition in 2004 with the opening of 'Locomotion', the NRM in Shildon, part of which is built around a historic site including the former workshop of steam locomotive engineer Timothy Hackworth (1786-1850). Hackworth was born at Wylam near Newcastle-upon-Tyne (coincidentally also the birthplace of George Stephenson, with whom he was later to work on the designs for early steam locos). He lived in Shildon and became the first Locomotive Superintendent for the Stockton & Darlington Railway. He later entered his 0-4-0 loco *Sans Pareil* in the 'Rainhill Trials' of 1829, and though it 'failed' on the day, its potential was recognised (largely due to its use of Hackworth's own invention of the 'blast-pipe', which recycles waste steam from the cylinders to increase the draught of the fire). The locomotive was bought by the Liverpool & Manchester Railway Company, later to be sold on to the Bolton & Leigh Railway, where it worked until 1844. A replica of *Sans Pareil* built in 1980 is preserved by the NRM at 'Locomotion', Shildon, with what remains of the original locomotive.

The 'Railfest' concept was also launched in 2004 with a nine-day festival at the NRM from Saturday 29 May to Sunday 6 June to celebrate 200 years of steam railways, the bicentenary of Richard Trevithick's first steam locomotive, which had pulled a train from Pen-y-Darren Ironworks at Merthyr Tydfil to Canal Basin at Abercynon on 21 February 1804, and the centenary of *City of Truro*'s record-setting 100mph run.

The UK RAILFEST 2004

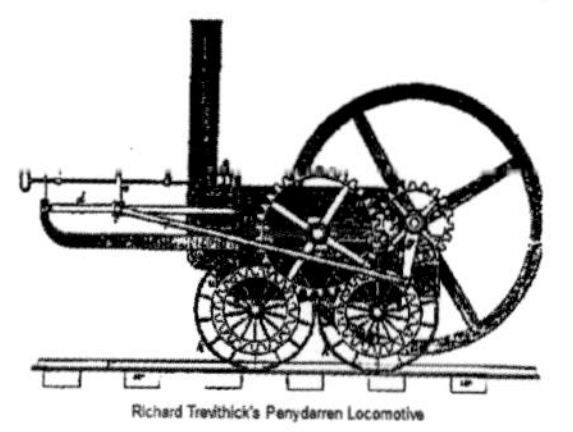

Richard Trevithick's Penydarren Locomotive

To be held at The National Railway Museum, York

Between May 29th & June 6th 2004

Commemorating the 200th Anniversary of the

Running of the World's First Steam Locomotive

Being admired by visitors outside the NRM on 2 June 2004 are Class 'B12' No 61572, 9F No 92203 and Class 84 electric No 84001.

Above: **No 61572 is the sole surviving member of the once 70-strong 'B12' Class 4-6-0s built for the Great Eastern Railway (GER) from 1911. Originally GER Class 'S69' (or the '1500' Class, as they became known), they were withdrawn between 1948 and 1953. No 61572 is owned by the Midland & Great Northern Joint Railway Society and is based on the North Norfolk Railway, in an area where members of the class were often seen at work.**

Right: **LNER Class 'K1' 2-6-0 No 62005 *Lord of the Isles* was built by the North British Locomotive Company in Glasgow in 1949 and withdrawn from service in 1967. Fortunately she was bought by a consortium, initially for spares for their 'K4' Class No 61994 *The Great Marquess*, but was not needed for that purpose and was therefore donated to the infant North Eastern Locomotive Preservation Group in 1972. After a thorough overhaul she featured for a time on the North Yorkshire Moors Railway before being put to work on main-line excursions, notably the 'Jacobite' rail tours over the West Highland Line from Fort William to Mallaig, operated by West Coast Railways.**

Right: **Needing little introduction, Gresley's famous 'A3' Class 4-6-2 No 4472 *Flying Scotsman* was built in 1927 at Doncaster for the LNER. She ran on BR as No 60103 until her 'retirement' in 1963, and following an enormously varied and much-travelled career she is now owned by the National Railway Museum.**

Some 70,000 visitors flocked in over the nine days to see the locos assembled for the occasion, which included such famous names as GWR 'City' Class 4-4-0 No 3440 *City of Truro* herself, Sir Nigel Gresley's much-travelled 'A3' 'Pacific' No 4472 *Flying Scotsman*, making a welcome return to Yorkshire, LMS 'Duchess' No 6233 *Duchess of Sutherland*, BR 'Britannia' Class No 70013 *Oliver Cromwell*, David Shepherd's 9F 2-10-0 No 92203 *Black Prince* and more modern 'classics' such as 'Deltic' No D9009 *Alycidon* and Virgin Trains' new 'Pendolino'.

Right: **LSWR Class '0298' 2-4-0WT No 30587 was built by Beyer Peacock in Manchester in 1874, and rebuilt by Adams (1884-92), then by Urie (1921-22), and finally by Maunsell (between 1931 and 1935). Known as the Beattie Well Tank, 85 locos were built for work in the suburbs of London and later on rural services throughout the South West of England. Most were withdrawn between 1886 and 1899 and subsequently scrapped, but three were retained to work on the Wenford branch in Cornwall and survived into the BR era, being finally condemned in 1962. Two of these have been preserved, with No 30587, owned by the NRM, being loaned to work on the Bodmin & Wenford Railway, while sister loco No 30585 is owned by the Quainton Railway Society and normally operates at its Buckinghamshire Railway Centre.**

Below left: **Stanier LMS 'Coronation' Class 4-6-2 No 6233 *Duchess of Sutherland* was outshopped from Crewe Works in July 1938. Following her career hauling Anglo-Scottish express services on the West Coast Main Line, during which time she ran 1,650,000 miles, she was withdrawn in February 1964. After a time spent at Butlins holiday camp at Heads-of-Ayr in Scotland, she was moved to Bressingham Steam Museum before being restored to full working condition at the Midland Railway Centre, Butterley. She can now be seen on main-line excursions once more.**

Below right: **BR Class 9F 2-10-0 No 92203 *Black Prince* was one of 251 heavy freight locomotives built for BR from 1954, including the last loco to be built, No 92220 *Evening Star*, in 1960, which is now preserved as part of the National Collection. No 92203 was built in January 1959 and withdrawn in November 1967, a working life of less than nine years. She was bought by the artist David Shepherd for £3,000, named *Black Prince* and moved to the Longmoor Military Railway until its closure in 1969, whereupon she spent some time at Eastleigh Depot before transferring to work on the East Somerset Railway. She is currently based on the North Norfolk Railway, being on loan there from the Gloucestershire Warwickshire Railway.**

This 'Railfest' line-up includes SR 'King Arthur' 'N15' Class 4-6-0 No 30777 *Sir Lamiel*, one of 30 built by the North British Locomotive Company in Glasgow from 1925 and withdrawn in 1961. She is owned by the NRM as part of the National Collection, and operated by the 5305 Locomotive Association, based at the Great Central Railway, Loughborough. Alongside her is *Black Prince*, and finally comes preserved Class 84 electric loco No 84001, introduced in 1960 as No E3036 for work on the newly electrified West Coast Main Line. She was one of only 10 built by the North British Locomotive Company and is the only one to survive into preservation, being withdrawn in 1979 and joining the National Collection. She is on loan to the AC Locomotive Group and housed at Barrow Hill Engine Shed, Staveley, Chesterfield.

'Railfest 2012' – undoubtedly *the* railway event of 2012

Eight years later the successful formula was repeated in the form of 'Railfest 2012', taking as its theme 'Record Breakers' and featuring such attractions as the HST power car No 43159, which is a joint holder of the diesel rail speed record, in company with GWR '3700' Class No 3440 *City of Truro*, widely accepted as the first steam locomotive to travel in excess of 100mph, achieved between Plymouth and London Paddington on 9 May 1904. Also on display was LNER Class 'A4' No 4468 *Mallard*, holder of the world steam record for a steam locomotive of 125.88mph set on Stoke Bank

Better known as No 4472 or No 60103, former LNER 'A3' *Flying Scotsman* is seen here in 'Wartime Black' while undergoing restoration. Built in 1923 for the LNER at Doncaster Works, her long career has seen her cover more than 2 million miles. While in service with the LNER, then BR, she was employed on long-distance express trains between London and Edinburgh, notably the 10.00am service from King's Cross, the 'Flying Scotsman', after which she was named. She was retired in 1963 and sold for preservation to Alan Pegler, who had her restored to LNER condition at Doncaster. Later, following her varied and much-travelled life, which included trips to the USA and Australia, she was eventually bought by the National Railway Museum in 2004 to become part of the National Collection. She is due to be returned to LNER 'Apple Green' livery following her overhaul.

near Grantham on 3 July 1938

'Railfest 2012', between Saturday 2 and Sunday 10 June was billed as 'the biggest show in the museum's history', and featured more than 50 locos, many of them record-breakers; it was expected to attract in the region of 65,000 visitors over the nine days. The main buildings of the NRM remained open with free entry as usual, but the yards and running tracks were the venue for this impressive gathering of steam and diesel locomotives. I visited on Tuesday 5 June, paid my £15 entry fee 'on the

Above: **'Princess Coronation' Class No 6229 (BR No 46229) *Duchess of Hamilton* was built at Crewe Works in 1938 as the last of the second batch of 'streamliners'. She was saved from scrapping with classmate No 46233 *Duchess of Sutherland* by Sir Billy Butlin, who bought them as children's playground exhibits for his holiday camps. A third 'Coronation' Class loco, No 46235 *City of Birmingham*, has also been preserved. Ownership of No 6229 passed to the National Railway Museum in 1987 after a period on loan, and she ran as the museum's flagship loco on main-line duties until 1996, when her boiler ticket expired. Since then she has been on static display at the NRM. She was returned to her original streamlined appearance in 2009, the work being carried out at Tyseley Locomotive Works, and there are plans to return her to steam in the near future.**

Left: **Furness Railway No 20, based at 'Locomotion', Shildon, is the oldest working standard-gauge steam locomotive in Britain, having been built in 1863 by Sharp, Stewart & Company, Manchester, to haul iron ore and slate trains to Barrow-in-Furness. She was preserved and restored to full working order by the Furness Railway Trust in 1999. Before arriving at the NRM for 'Railfest 2012', No 20 had been on a tour that included appearances at the Severn Valley Railway, the Ribble Steam Railway in Preston and the Midland Railway at Butterley. Leaving York, she returned to 'Locomotion' after putting in a guest appearance at the Middleton Railway in Leeds for its gala to mark 200 years of commercial steam haulage on this historic preserved line.**

0-4-0ST No 2012 *Teddy*, built in 1941 by Peckett & Sons at Albion Works, Bristol, is seen here giving rides aboard the Derwent Valley Light Railway's restored coach 'Sylvia' and SR guards van No 56297. Her usual home is on the 'Lavender Line', a short standard-gauge heritage railway near Uckfield in East Sussex.

door' and enjoyed a thoroughly 'special' day among the locos and fellow enthusiasts. Food and drink outlets provided sustenance, while music from a jazz band created an almost 'party' atmosphere for the occasion. To cap it all, even the sun made a welcome appearance in what was otherwise a generally dull, cold and wet early summer.

LMS 'Jubilee' Class No 45596 *Bahamas* was built in 1935 by the North British Locomotive Company in Glasgow. Withdrawn in July 1966, she was bought by the newly formed Bahamas Locomotive Society, creator of the Dinting Railway Museum near Glossop, Derbyshire. The museum closed in 1991, whereupon the society and its collection moved to a new base at Ingrow West railway station on the Keighley & Worth Valley Railway. Alongside *Bahamas* is BR Class 31 diesel No 31601, one of a class of 263 Brush Type 2 locomotives built by Brush Traction between 1957 and 1962. Currently operational, she is seen here in the livery of Devon & Cornwall Railways (DCR), a subsidiary of the train operating company British American Railway Services (BARS), which specialises in loco and rolling stock hire and maintenance. BARS also owns diesel loco No 56312, which was also on display at 'Railfest 2012'.

Top: GWR No 3717 (3440) *City of Truro*, designed by George Jackson Churchward and built at Swindon Works in 1903, is famous as being the first steam locomotive to achieve a speed in excess of 100mph, which she did while descending Wellington Bank, Somerset, at the head of the 'Ocean Mails' special from Plymouth to London Paddington on 9 May 1904. Retired from regular service in 1931, *City of Truro* was donated to and preserved at the LNER Railway Museum, York, following the refusal of the Directors of the GWR to preserve her at their company's expense. Unusually, she was returned to service on BR Western Region in 1957, hauling special excursions as well as normal revenue services. She was retired a second time in 1961, at which time she was renumbered back to 3717 and housed at Swindon's GWR Museum until 1984, when she was moved to the NRM, York. Following major restoration in 2004, marking the 100th anniversary of her record-breaking run, she is now based at the Gloucestershire Warwickshire Railway, though she frequently visits other UK heritage railways.

Centre: Class 56 diesel No 56312 is in DCR grey and silver livery, with York NRM 'Railfest 2012' advertising. She is currently operational and can be seen on Colas Rail steel trains and container workings, as well as featuring on excursions from time to time.

Bottom: The Class 92 electric locos were designed specifically to operate the Channel Tunnel services between England and France. Built between 1993 and 1999, 46 locos are operated by Eurotunnel and DB Schenker, while in France a number are also owned and operated by SNCF, where they are known as the CC 92000 Class. No 92032 is operated by Eurotunnel and has been outshopped in blue and yellow GBRf/Eurotunnel livery, unlike all the other Eurotunnel locos, which are in British Rail two-tone grey.

Left: **Working on a painting depicting 'A4' No 60007 *Sir Nigel Gresley* alongside 'A1' No 60163 *Tornado* is Guild of Railway Artists member David Charlesworth. One of two such artists working on the day, he is on board a former SR goods wagon now restored as 'Open Passenger Wagon' No 1758 of the Middleton Colliery, Leeds.**

Below: **Perhaps appropriately positioned together are Gresley's 'A4' 'Pacific' No 4468 *Mallard* and 'Deltic' No 55002 *The King's Own Yorkshire Light Infantry*. No 4468 was built at Doncaster in 1938 and achieved fame and historical significance by becoming the holder of the official world speed record for steam locomotives, at 125.88mph, reached on the slight downward grade of Stoke Bank on the ECML near Grantham on 3 July 1938. When retired in 1963 she had covered almost 1½ million miles, and though restored to working order in the 1980s was only lightly used on occasional 'specials'. She now resides at the National Railway Museum as part of the National Collection. 'Deltic' No 55002, affectionately known as 'KOYLI', represents the successors to the 'A3s' and 'A4s'. Introduced from 1961, they took over the handling of the Anglo-Scottish expresses on the ECML and forced the steam locos into retirement. Now also part of the National Collection, No 55002 hauled her last train, a Liverpool to York service, on 30 December 1981, after which she took up her position in the Great Hall of the NRM. Following a time with the Deltic Preservation Society (DPS) at Barrow Hill, where she was cosmetically restored, she was returned to working order in 2011 at the NRM, following a successful appeal for funding.**

12. Steam still special

Introduced by the LNER in 1936, Gresley-designed 'V2' No 60800 *Green Arrow* pauses at York station in May 2003 with a charter special for Scarborough.

Of one thing, however, there is no doubt – in spite of all the changes, steam has prevailed, and the years following 2000 have seen no let up in the number or the popularity of steam-hauled excursions, while at the same time the heritage railway centres continue to draw the crowds.

According to information provided by AbRail Rail Databases, which lists all the steam locomotives in preservation that were manufactured by BR, as well as those of the pre- and post-Grouping companies and the War Department (WD), at 30 June 2012 there were 493 preserved steam locos in the UK. Of these, 186 are listed as 'Active', 110 as 'Display', 122 undergoing restoration or overhaul, and 54 being in storage; the remaining few are currently overseas or, in the case of a couple of examples, 'not known'. The main sources of these preserved locos are given as: GWR 117,

Top: **At York station on 6 July 2005 the world-famous *Flying Scotsman* hauls the 'Scarborough Spa Express', with barely an 'enthusiast' in sight. *Douglas Todd***

Centre: **The year 2007 saw the founding of a charity to raise money to provide help for wounded, injured and sick service personnel, veterans and their families. From modest beginnings, the 'Help for Heroes' campaign touched a nerve with the British public and fast became a national phenomenon, with fund-raising events being staged throughout the country in support of the wounded. One such was the 'Help for Heroes' special steam charter, seen here passing Colton Junction on the approach to York on 27 March 2010, when Stanier 8F No 48151 and BR 'Britannia' 'Pacific' No 70013 *Oliver Cromwell* (running as No 70048 *The Territorial Army 1908-2008*) ran from Lancaster to York in aid of this worthy cause. *Douglas Todd***

Bottom: **LMS 'Jubilee' No 5690 *Leander* takes the 'Scarborough Spa Express' away from York on 29 July 2008, in the days when the journey went to Leeds before returning to York via Harrogate and thence onward to Scarborough.**

LMS 92, LNER 39, and SR 80. A further 52 are listed as ex-WD and 88 as having been produced during the BR years, i.e. from 1948 onwards. The remainder originate from narrow-gauge or privately owned railways.

And there is of course the continuing lure of main-line steam – with York as always at the forefront. The city, as befits a great railway centre of such long standing, continues to attract those who come in search of steam power. Throughout the summer months a regular programme of tours that either originate here, or feature York as a destination or major pick-up point, keep the enthusiasts and casual admirers alike well supplied with a feast of lovingly restored reminders of that bygone age. In addition, special 'one-off' charters add further interest and occasional poignancy to the steam calendar.

Locos representing the former LMS have featured heavily on the main line in York since the turn of the century, with 'Jubilee' No 5690 *Leander* working regularly on the 'Scarborough Spa Express', running three days per week

Above: **LMS 'Princess Royal' Class No 6201 *Princess Elizabeth* races through Church Fenton heading for York with the Crewe to Scarborough and return 'Scarborough Flyer' on 23 July 2010.**

Below left: **A quartet of 'Scarborough Spa Expresses': here 'Royal Scot' Class No 46115 *Scots Guardsman* heads for the coast from York on 2 August 2011.**

Below right: **'Black 5' No 45407 takes the route towards Wakefield on 19 July 2011, bizarrely carrying a 'Flying Scotsman' headboard.**

Bottom left: **'Britannia' Class No 70013 *Oliver Cromwell* is captured at speed through Colton Junction heading for York on 30 August 2011.**

Bottom Right: **'Black 5' No 44932 passes Towthorpe Crossings near York en route for Scarborough on 23 October 2011.**

Right: **Heading another York-based 'favourite', 'Black 5' No 45407 races through Long Preston on 24 July 2011 at the head of 'The Waverley' excursion from York to Carlisle via the Settle and Carlisle line. Built by Armstrong Whitworth in Newcastle during 1937, she survived to the last days of steam in August 1968, to be housed at 'Steamtown', Carnforth, for some years before moving to her current home on the East Lancashire Railway.**

Below right: **One of the two remaining examples of Stanier's 'Princess Royal' Class, or 'Lizzies' as they were affectionately known, No 6201 *Princess Elizabeth*, is seen at work with the Crewe to Scarborough and return 'Scarborough Flyer' near Haxby, between York and Malton, on 9 September 2011. Built at Crewe in 1933, she was withdrawn in 1962 after a career hauling some of the fastest and heaviest trains on the West Coast Main Line between London Euston and Glasgow, to be bought and saved by the Princess Elizabeth Locomotive Society, and is now based at Crewe Heritage Centre. The other remaining example of the class is sister loco No 46203 *Princess Margaret Rose*, built at Crewe in 1935 and withdrawn after a similar career to her other classmates in 1962. *Princess Margaret Rose* is owned by the Princess Royal Class Preservation Trust and is based at the Midland Railway Centre, Butterley.**

during July and August, and 'Princess Royal' No 6201 *Princess Elizabeth* operating the 'Scarborough Flyer' on Fridays.

Since 2010 gauging problems on the 'Harrogate Loop', which put a stop to steam locomotives taking that route, have meant that the 'Scarborough Spa Express' has used the 'Wakefield Circle' instead. This involves the trains setting off in the morning from York to travel to Wakefield via Normanton, then to Castleford and back to York, before setting out for Scarborough as usual, to return to York in the afternoon before completing the 'Wakefield Circle' a second time.

Stanier's 'Pacifics', arguably among the cream of steam locomotives ever to have graced our tracks, have sadly not survived in any numbers. Of his 'Princess Royal' Class, introduced from 1933, only two of the 13 have been preserved, and from the later 'Princess Coronation' Class, which many regard as his crowning glory, only three survive from the 38 produced.

Of Stanier's 'Princess Coronation' Class, or 'Duchesses' as they were often known, built between 1937 and 1948 at Crewe Works, the survivors include No (4)6233 *Duchess of Sutherland*, built at Crewe in 1938 and now owned by the Princess Royal Class Locomotive Trust, and No 46203 *Princess Margaret Rose*,

Top: **As well as being a regular performer on the 'Scarborough Flyer', No 6201 *Princess Elizabeth* was in demand for other duties on the main line during 2011. Here she is seen at Colton Junction, York, working the return 'Yorkshire Coronation' Sheffield-York-Scarborough tour on 21 May.**

Centre: **No 6201 was a featured loco on the series of 'shuttles' organised between the National Railway Museum's York and Shildon centres during September 2011. She is seen here passing Shipton by Beningbrough near York on the 18th, under threatening skies. Other locos involved in the shuttles were Stanier 'Black 5' No 45305, GWR 'Hall' No 5972 *Olton Hall*, Class 47 diesel No 47798 and Class 37 diesel No 37706.**

Bottom: **'Princess Coronation' Class No 6233 *Duchess of Sutherland* passes Railway Cottages Crossing on the East Coast Main Line north of York on 30 September 2010, with the second leg of the 'Silver Jubilee' excursion from London King's Cross to Newcastle. She is seen here outshopped in 'BR Lined Black' livery. The first leg, from King's Cross to York, had been hauled by Gresley 'A4' No 60019 *Bittern*.**

similarly based at the Midland Railway Centre, Butterley.

In addition to No 46233, the two other lucky survivors of the 'Princess Coronation' Class are No 46235 *City of Birmingham*, which is now on display at 'Think Tank', Birmingham's new Science Museum, following her removal from the now defunct former Birmingham Science Museum site, and No 46229 *Duchess*

Right: **Following a major overhaul at Butterley, and now sporting 'authentic Brunswick Green' livery as used by BR in the early 1950s and numbered 46233, she heads 'The Hadrian' south past the same crossing on 30 June 2012, heading for York after taking her train from Hellifield to Carlisle, then on to Hexham and Darlington.**

of Hamilton, which has been operational on main-line duties but is now on display at the NRM in her re-streamlined condition.

Not surprisingly in this part of the railway world, locomotives from the former LNER also feature prominently on main-line duties, with Gresley's 'A4' 'Pacifics' taking the lion's share of the work, ably supported by 'new recruit' *Tornado*. Sir Nigel Gresley (1876-1941) designed his streamlined 'A4' Class 'Pacific' locos while Chief Mechanical Engineer (CME) of the London & North Eastern Railway (LNER). Thirty-five were produced at Doncaster Works between 1935 and 1938 to haul express passenger trains between London King's Cross and Edinburgh. Nicknamed 'Streaks', most were withdrawn between 1962 and 1966 as they were replaced by the 'Deltic' diesel locomotives. The class included the famous *Mallard*, No 4468, official holder of the record for the fastest steam loco in the world.

Above right: **Taking a turn with the inaugural 'Scarborough Flyer' of 2012, now routed from Tyseley to Scarborough and return, No 46233 heads back to York from Scarborough on 30 June 2012.**

Right: **The re-streamlined No 46229 *Duchess of Hamilton* on display in the NRM.**

'A4' No 60019 *Bittern*, with two tenders, heads south from York past Colton Junction en route for King's Cross with 'The Great Britain III' rail tour on 14 April 2010. Earlier, the first leg of this journey from Edinburgh to York had been brought in by LMS 'Princess Royal' Class No 46201 *Princess Elizabeth*.

Six of the class have been preserved, four of them in the UK. They are Nos 4464 (BR No 60019) *Bittern*, 4468 (60022) *Mallard*, 4488 (60009) *Union of South Africa* and 4498 (60007) *Sir Nigel Gresley*. Two more are at present abroad, both on static display, Nos 4489 (60010) *Dominion of Canada*, based at the Canadian Railway Museum, and 4496 (60008) *Dwight D. Eisenhower*, at the National Railroad Museum in Green Bay, Wisconsin, USA. Both the North American 'A4s' were brought to the National Railway Museum in York in 2012 on a two-year loan, so reuniting all six survivors

'A4' No 60007 *Sir Nigel Gresley* races towards York near Colton Junction on the King's Cross to Newcastle Christmas 'Tynesider' of 18 December 2010.

Running as 'A4' No 4492 *Dominion of New Zealand*, No 60019 *Bittern* hauls the King's Cross to Tyne Yard portion of the 'Great Britain IV' rail tour on 16 April 2011, passing Shipton by Beningbrough, north of York. The final section of the journey on to Edinburgh was taken by No 60007 *Sir Nigel Gresley*.

to celebrate the 75th anniversary of *Mallard*'s record-breaking run with a series of events during the summer of 2013.

Class 'A1' 'new-build' loco No 60163 *Tornado* was outshopped from Darlington Works in 2008, having been built by the A1 Steam Locomotive Trust. None of the original Peppercorn 'A1' series of 49 locos built during the late 1940s has survived into preservation.

Perhaps it should come as no surprise that locos from the former Southern Railway and the Great Western Railway are not well represented among the haulers of steam 'specials' around the York area, and when they

Passing Overton, on the East Coast Main Line north of York, 'A1' No 60163 is towing 'A4' No 4468 *Mallard* from the NRM for display at 'Locomotion', the NRM at Shildon, on 23 June 2010.

Above: **In the beautiful late-afternoon sunlight of 24 November 2011, No 60163 *Tornado* restarts from a signal check at Colton Junction on the approach to York with the King's Cross to York 'Cathedrals Express', already running 2 hours late.**

Below right: **A rare visitor to Yorkshire is former Southern Railway 'Battle of Britain' Class 'Light Pacific' No 34067 *Tangmere*, seen here with the inaugural 'Scarborough Flyer' of 22 July 2011, approaching Colton Junction near York. Built at Brighton for the Southern Railway in 1947, *Tangmere* was one of a class of 110 built between 1945 and 1951 to a design by CME Oliver Bulleid. However, problems associated with adhesion, maintenance issues and high fuel consumption led BR to order the rebuilding of 60 of the class between 1957 and 1961. This solved many of their problems, but the remaining 50 locos, *Tangmere* included, were never rebuilt and continued in their 'unrebuilt' 'air-smoothed' state until their withdrawal from service in the 1960s. Twenty members of the class have been preserved and several have been restored to operational condition, being based on heritage railways including the Mid Hants, Bluebell, Severn Valley, Swanage, Great Central, West Somerset, Nene Valley, Keighley & Worth Valley and North Yorkshire Moors. *Tangmere* was withdrawn from service in 1963 and sent to Woodham's scrapyard in South Wales to be cut up, from where she was rescued and eventually restored to full main-line running condition. She is currently based at West Coast Railways' Southall depot.**

Left: **Former GWR 'Hall' Class No 5972 *Olton Hall*, aka *Hogwarts Castle*, hauls LNER 'A4' No 4468 *Mallard* between NRM Shildon and NRM York on 19 July 2011. Built at Swindon in 1937, No 5972 was withdrawn from service in December 1963 and sent for scrapping to Woodham's yard at Barry Dock, from where she eventually became rescue No 125 in May 1981.**

Below: **At Colton Junction, York, on 18 December 2010, 'Castle' No 5043 *Earl of Mount Edgcumbe* arrives with the Tyseley to York 'Christmas White Rose'.**

appear on Yorkshire metals they never fail to impress.

Two former Great Western Railway locos have become regular sights in the York area. Alnwick Castle was used in the 'Harry Potter' films to depict the magical Hogwarts Castle, and the 'Hogwarts Express', which carries students from London King's Cross to Hogsmead station, was filmed partly on the North Yorkshire Moors Railway, so the locomotive featured in the series, No 5972 *Olton Hall*, disguised as *Hogwarts Castle*, has become quite a local celebrity, based as she now is at the NRM, Shildon.

No 5043 passes the same location a year later, on 17 December 2011, at the head of the same excursion.

The second of the GWR 'visitors' is the more conventional 'Castle' Class locomotive No 5043 *Earl of Mount Edgcumbe*, built at Swindon in March 1936 to a design by Collett, and originally named *Barbury Castle*, being renamed in 1937. No 5043 is one of eight 'Castle' Class locos to have been preserved from the original 171 built between 1923 and 1950 at Swindon Works. The other survivors are Nos 4073 *Caerphilly Castle*, 4079 *Pendennis Castle*, 5029 *Nunney Castle*, 5051 *Earl Bathurst* (originally *Drysllwyn Castle*), 5080 *Defiant* (formerly *Ogmore Castle*), 7027 *Thornbury Castle* and 7029 *Clun Castle*.

No 5043 *Earl of Mount Edgcumbe* was withdrawn from service in December 1963 and again sent to Woodham's scrapyard, from where she was bought by the then Birmingham Railway Museum at Tyseley. There she was kept in store, initially to act as a source of spares for classmate No 7029 *Clun Castle*, but was later restored in her own right, achieving main-line operational standard in October 2008.

Not to be outdone by the 'Big Four', BR's own 'Standard' designs have given a good account of themselves in recent times, with 'Britannia' Nos 70000 and 70013 much in evidence, together with the 'one-off' Class 8P 4-6-2 No 71000 *Duke of Gloucester*, whose long-awaited return has been another success story in the annals of steam preservation.

'Britannia' Class No 70013 *Oliver Cromwell* hurries towards York at Colton Junction with a charter from King's Cross on 17 December 2011, not long after 'Castle' No 5043 *Earl of Mount Edgcumbe* had passed with her train from Tyseley. Incidentally, both excursions were entitled 'The Christmas White Rose'.

Duke of Gloucester is owned and operated by the 71000 (Duke of Gloucester) Steam Locomotive Trust Ltd, which restored her from scrapyard to 'as built' condition following her withdrawal in 1962, after only eight years in service. The brainchild of Robert Riddles, CME for BR and responsible for overseeing the design of the 'Standard' classes. When built in 1954 'the Duke' was intended to be the forerunner of a new breed of modern express locomotives embodying the

Above: **No 70013 is seen in action again on the East Coast Main Line, here passing Shipton by Beningbrough at the head of 'The Tynesider', a Cleethorpes to Morpeth excursion, on 10 March 2012. This loco achieved fame when, on 11 August 1968, she was selected as one of the four to haul the last BR steam passenger train prior to the abolition of steam traction on BR, the legendary 'Fifteen Guinea Special', from Liverpool to Carlisle. She is now part of the National Collection.**

Left: **Sister loco No 70000 *Britannia*, when built at Crewe Works in January 1951, was the first of BR's 'Standard' locos and the first of a class of 55 built between 1951 and 1954. Though No 70000 was withdrawn in May 1966, other members of the class outlived her in service and survived to the end of steam in 1968, being the only 'Pacific' locos so to do. She is currently owned by the Royal Scot Locomotive and General Trust and based at the LNWR Heritage Workshops, Crewe. She is seen here heading towards York on the East Coast Main Line on a move from Grosmont (North Yorkshire Moors Railway) to Southall (West Coast Railways) on 16 May 2012.**

Right: **BR Class 8P 4-6-2 No 71000 *Duke of Gloucester* passes Colton Junction on 19 May 2011 with the York to Carlisle leg of the 'Cumbrian Mountain Express'.**

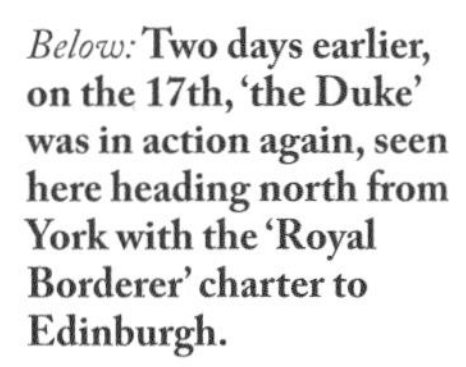

Below: **Two days earlier, on the 17th, 'the Duke' was in action again, seen here heading north from York with the 'Royal Borderer' charter to Edinburgh.**

latest developments in steam technology. However, the costs involved in her production proved prohibitive, and with the advent of the 1955 Modernisation Plan, with its emphasis firmly on the electrification of main lines and the replacement of the steam fleet by diesel locomotives, the project was scrapped, leaving the prototype 'Duke' as the only one of its kind ever constructed.

The summer months from June to September have traditionally been a period of intense activity for railway enthusiasts, being the season of holidays and, hopefully, fine weather, allowing an opportunity to explore with increased enthusiasm what is on offer from the tour operators and railway centres, an opportunity that those in the business of marketing railway nostalgia have not been slow to exploit, as a glance at the published lists of UK rail tours involving steam traction will confirm. The numbers for the summer months of 2012 were 39 in June, 62 in July, 71 in August, and 59 in September – and these figures do not include non-steam-hauled excursions, of which there are many each month.

Among this plethora of opportunities for lovers of steam 'specials' are those that run

Stanier 'Black 5' No 44932 is a regular at the head of the 'Scarborough Spa Express', and is seen here shortly after leaving York, approaching Towthorpe Crossings on its way to Scarborough on 15 August 2012.

on a regular weekly basis during the summer season, and feature York in the itinerary, including 'The Scarborough Flyer' (usually Crewe-Scarborough) and 'The Waverley' (York-Carlisle). In addition there are those excursions that run even more regularly, such as 'The Cathedrals Express', operated by Steam Dreams, which, as its name suggests, visits important cities such as York on its tours, which are usually twice weekly, and West Coast Railways' 'The Scarborough Spa Express', which begins in York and visits Wakefield and Castleford, then back to York, before setting off for Scarborough, then returning to York to repeat the Wakefield/Castleford loop once more. The latter leaves York at 10.14 and does not end its day's work until 20.56 – quite a testing time for loco and crew, which they do every Tuesday, Wednesday and Thursday between mid-July and the end of August.

With this number of rail tours it seems inevitable that on occasions there will simply be too many events chasing too few customers, with the result that some have to be cancelled due to insufficient support. This was certainly the case during 2012, especially for mid-week excursions. Nevertheless, the pool of steam locomotives available for these tours remains impressive, both in terms of number and variety. They include, from the GWR, favourites such as Nos 4965 *Rood Ashton Hall*, 5043 *Earl of Mount Edgcumbe*, 3850, 7752, 9466 and 9600, and from the SR Nos 30777 *Sir Lamiel*, 34067 *Tangmere* and 35028 *Clan Line*. The LMS is well represented, with 'Black 5' Nos 44871, 44932, 45305 and 45407 being employed regularly, together with Nos 46115 *Scots Guardsman*, 8F 48151, 46201 *Princess Elizabeth* and 46233 *Duchess of Sutherland*. From the LNER come 'A4' Nos 60009 *Union of South Africa* and 60019 *Bittern*, No 61994 *The Great Marquess*, No 62005 and of course 'new-build' No 60163 *Tornado*. Nor must we forget BR locos Nos 70000 *Britannia*, 70013 *Oliver Cromwell* and 71000 *Duke of Gloucester*.

In fact, by 2012 a total of 105 preserved steam locomotives had been allocated five-digit TOPS numbers to allow them to operate over the national network, though not all of these may be currently authorised for use on Network Rail metals – all this in addition to the numerous heritage railways up and down the country that add summer special events to their normal running timetables, providing opportunities virtually every day to satisfy the cravings of even the most demanding chaser of trains.

In particular, the combination of three summer 'regulars' in the York means that main-line steam operates through the city on no fewer than five days each week. Tour operator West Coast Railways runs the popular York-based steam tour the 'Scarborough Spa Express'. During 2012 this excursion worked the route three times each week from 17 July to

Above: **Though there are plans to return 'Princess Coronation' Class No 6229 (BR 46229)** ***Duchess of Hamilton*** **to steam in the future, no time scale has yet been released for this to take place. In the meantime sister loco No 46233** ***Duchess of Sutherland*****, seen here, carries the torch for Stanier's flagship class. She is heading the Crewe-Scarborough 'Scarborough Flyer' at Colton Junction on the outskirts of York on 17 August 2012.**

Below: **After a brief signal check, 'The Duchess' gets 'The Flyer' on its way again at Bolton Percy on the approach to York on 31 August 2012.** ***Rick Ward***

30 August, making good use of one of Stanier's ex-LMS workhorses, 'Black 5' Nos 44932, 45305 or 45407, 'Royal Scot' No 46115 *Scots Guardsman*, or 8F No 48151.

Though it must be said that in recent years the variety of traction provided for the 'Scarborough Spa Express' has been limited, this was not always the case, as a look at the impressive list of famous names that have carried the now familiar headboard will reveal. Locos involved have included Nos 3440 *City of Truro*, 777 *Sir Lamiel*, 34092 *City of Wells*, 5690 *Leander*, 4472 *Flying Scotsman*, 4498 *Sir Nigel Gresley*, 4771 *Green Arrow*, 60009 *Union of South Africa* and 92220 *Evening Star*.

One of the most popular steam rail tours in recent years, certainly in the North of England, has been the regular Sunday excursion from York to Carlisle and return by way of the always impressive Settle and Carlisle line. Promoted by the Railway Touring Company, 'The Waverley' runs from late July until early September, picking

Above: **No 48151 is seen here at the head of the 'Scarborough Spa Express' once more, speeding away from York towards the east coast town on 23 August 2012.**

Right: **The following week saw the last runs of the train for the 2012 season, and on 30 August 'Black 5' No 45305 is seen racing past Towthorpe Crossings, east of York, with the very last one of the year. The coach behind the loco is ex-BR Inspectors Saloon No 999506, built at Wolverton in 1957.**

Below: **No 45305 storms past Colton Junction for the final time, minus headboard, with the evening trip to Wakefield and back from York.**

Above and right: **Stanier 'Black 5' No 44932 has charge of 'The Waverley' on 26 August 2012. She is seen waiting at York station, where her driver gives an impatient look back, eager to be away.**

up at Leeds then heading out via Keighley and Skipton to join the famous 'Long Drag' at Settle Junction.

A water stop at Hellifield tops up the tender before the train attacks the 1 in 100 climb through Horton-in-Ribblesdale and onwards to cross the mighty Ribblehead Viaduct, before plunging into the darkness of Blea Moor Tunnel, which runs some 500 feet below the wild fells for a distance of 1½ miles. Emerging at last into beautiful Dentdale gives a brief but welcome respite to the crew before the climb is resumed towards the summit at Ais Gill. A further water stop at Appleby is completed before the final cruise down the lovely Eden Valley to the border city of Carlisle. A 2-hour stay here allows time to explore this historic city before the return trip tackles the testing gradient once more.

All this combines to make for an attractive and varied day out for the railway enthusiast, which starts with breakfast on the train as it accelerates away from York shortly after 9.00am and ends as darkness falls at around 8.30pm – an exhilarating experience that is highly recommended.

The third member of York's 'summer steam

No 44932 speeds past Colton Junction towards Leeds on the first leg of the journey to Carlisle. ***Rick Ward***

Left: **At Carlisle station 'Black 5' No 44932 poses for photographers after an exhilarating journey over the demanding Settle and Carlisle route on 26 August 2012. Loco and crew are due a well-earned rest before tackling the 'Long Drag' again, but in the opposite direction.**

Above: **The beautifully restored Pullman Restaurant Car 'Emerald' provides an added touch of elegance.**

Below: **The return water stop at Appleby is efficiently completed before we charge southwards once more, passing Pen-y-Ghent, near Horton-in-Ribblesdale.**

trio' is 'The Scarborough Flyer', which occupies the Friday slot. Also from the Railway Touring Company stable, this Crewe to Scarborough and return working featured, for the 2012 season, 'Princess Coronation' Class No 46233 *Duchess of Sutherland*, designed by Sir William A. Stanier and built at Crewe in 1938 for the LMS, or Sir Nigel Gresley's 'A4' No 60009 *Union of South Africa*, built at Doncaster in 1937 for the LNER. Each was guaranteed to give full value and, in late summer sunshine, both looked at their splendid best.

As the summer of 2012 drew to a close, so too did another steam season. As usual at this autumn time, trackside opportunities are often limited to other traction, with steam being the exception rather than the rule, until the 'festive season' brings their welcome return. It is worth noting here that at the time of writing, in addition to the more than 100 steam

Left: **At Hellifield, as at other strategic points along the route, groups of enthusiasts gather to record our passing.**

Below: **As the last light of the day gives way to evening, we arrive back at York, on time.**

locomotives mentioned earlier as having been allocated TOPS numbers for national network running, a total of 63 preserved 'modern traction' locos have also received such numbers for the same reason.

A rare event on 28 September 2012 saw the only surviving main-line-registered Class 87 electric loco, No 87002 *Royal Sovereign*, visit York at the head of 'The Modern Railways Golden Jubilee Special' from King's Cross to York and the

Above: **Passing the site of the former station at Bolton Percy on the approach to York, No 46233 *Duchess of Sutherland*, in 'BR Green', heads 'The Flyer' on 31 August 2012.**

Right: **At the same location a week later, on 7 September, 'A4' 'No 9' *Union of South Africa* has the honour.**

An unusual convoy passes Shipton on the approach to York on 18 September 2012, as 'Deltic' No 55022 *Royal Scots Grey* leads train 0Z52, a Grosmont to Barrow Hill loco move. Behind the 'Deltic' are diesel locos Nos 37275, 33108 and 47798, all of which had been involved at the North Yorkshire Moors Diesel Gala the previous weekend. The Class 47 was detached at York, while the remainder continued their journey. Later, at Barrow Hill, No 55022 was joined by classmates Nos 55002 *The King's Own Yorkshire Light Infantry* and 55019 *Royal Highland Fusilier* for the journey back to the East Lancashire Railway.

National Railway Museum, there to celebrate the naming of GBRf Class 66 No 66745 *Modern Railways: The First Fifty Years*, which would later haul the train back to London. The 35 BR Class 87/0 and sole Class 87/1 Bo-Bo locos were built at BREL Crewe between 1973 and 1975 to work the express passenger services over the newly electrified West Coast Main Line between London Euston and Glasgow. Only three of the class have been preserved in this country: No 87001 *Stephenson/Royal Scot* is at the NRM, York, on static display as part of the National Collection; No 87002 *Royal Sovereign* is preserved in main-line operational condition, owned by the AC Locomotive Group and based at Willesden Depot; and No 87 035 *Robert Burns* is preserved as a static exhibit at the Crewe Heritage Centre. Twelve of the locos have been scrapped, Nos 87005/11/15/16/18/21/24/27/30/31/32/36 (the latter subsequently allocated the number 87101 and named *Stephenson*, the only member of Class 87/1). The remaining locos have been sold and exported to work for the Bulgarian Railway Company.

The only remaining main-line-registered Class 87, No 87002 *Royal Sovereign*, approaches Colton Junction, York, with train 1Z87, 'The Modern Railways Golden Jubilee Special' from King's Cross, promoted by UK Railtours on 28 September 2012.

Through the fog on Saturday 24 November 2012 comes Gresley 'A4' 'Pacific' No 60009 *Union of South Africa*, hauling the sole-surviving steam portion of rail tour 1Z50, 'The Tynesider', from Newcastle to King's Cross and return, seen here (but only just!) heading south on the East Coast Main Line at Colton Junction, York. The Newcastle to York portion was to have been headed by sister loco No 60007 *Sir Nigel Gresley*, which was declared 'unavailable' at the last minute, having been 'failed' before the Newcastle to York leg. This resulted in what must have been a major disappointment for passengers when the train was hauled by Class 47 diesel No 47270 *Swift*, from the stock of West Coast Railways, which also brought back the return from King's Cross to Newcastle.

The end of the year signals the beginning of the winter 'specials' season. In 2012, after a steam 'drought' of more than a month, the prospect of not one but two of the preserved Gresley 'A4s' visiting York hauling 'The Tynesider' rail tour from Newcastle to King's Cross and return was certainly a mouth-watering prospect. The weather had predictably turned beyond the glorious colours of autumn to the unstable mix that is often characteristic of early winter, when mild south-westerlies bring rain and bitter northerlies sweep in hard on their heels. Such was to be the case on Saturday 24 November, when just such a mix was bringing chaos in the form of high winds, then flooding and finally, and worst of all, dense fog.

Over the years, the beautiful and historic City of York has earned itself a reputation as the place to visit over the Christmas period, which begins with the annual St Nicholas Fayre at the end of November. The Fayre specialises in local farm produce, hand-crafted goods and festive treats, with stall-holders in traditional Victorian costume offering these and other delights, including roast chestnuts, mulled wine and Christmas cake. The streets are decorated with festive lights and Christmas trees, and throng with locals and visitors enjoying the unique atmosphere, set against the backdrop of York's historic buildings and echoing to the majestic and uplifting peal of the Minster bells.

Not surprising, then, that the event attracts rail tours from the length and breadth of the country, starting in 2012 with a 'threesome' that brought hundreds of visitors on Saturday 1 December.

An infrequent yet welcome visitor put in an appearance at York on Tuesday and Wednesday 4 and 5 December 2012 in the form of the 'Northern Belle', with the 'Christmas Lunch' specials, aboard which guests 'enjoy fine food and wine as you set off on a round trip through Britain's glorious countryside'.

Meanwhile, within York's National Railway Museum work continued on major projects

The 2012 Christmas festivities in York got under way officially with the three-day St Nicholas Fayre, held in the city between 30 November and 2 December. The first of the three 'specials' bringing in visitors on Saturday 1 December was NENTA Train Tours' 'Yorkshire Christmas Festivities' rail tour, originating in Walsham, Norfolk, and featuring West Coast Railways' less than pristine Class 47 No 47760 'topping and tailing' with No 47854 *Diamond Jubilee*, seen here passing Colton Junction on the approach to York.

Next to pass the same location not long afterwards was UK Railtours' 'The St Nicholas Fayre in York' tour, which originated at London St Pancras and featured an East Midlands Trains HST set headed by No 43043, with No 43081 at the rear.

The third member of the trio, a fitting finale, appeared in the shape of Gresley 'A4' 'Pacific' No 60009 *Union of South Africa*, rounding the curve on the East Coast Main Line, chime whistle blowing, much to the delight of the 50 or so enthusiasts who had gathered at Colton Junction to witness these events. Here 'No 9' is seen heading the Railway Touring Company's 'The Christmas White Rose', in conditions that could not have been more different than those just a week before.

Right: **The 'Northern Belle' accelerates away from a signal check at Colton Junction on 4 December 2012, headed by No 47832 *Solway Princess*, with No 47501 *Craftsman* in DRS livery at the rear.**

Below right: **Not widely broadcast yet occurring on the same day was the light engine 'loco move' of Gresley 'K4' No 61994 *The Great Marquess* with its support coach from the National Railway Museum, York, to Crewe. Introduced in 1938 as one of only six such locos designed specifically for the testing conditions of Scotland's West Highland Line, five of the six were withdrawn in 1961. One, LNER No 3445, had been withdrawn as early as 1945 and was rebuilt as BR No 61997 *MacCailin Mor*, the first of the 'K1' Class. A further 70 were to follow from 1949. No 61994, the only 'K4' to survive into preservation, is seen here passing the site of the former station at Bolton Percy, between York and Leeds.**

Below: **'Deltic' No 55022/D9000 *Royal Scots Grey*, looking in need of a little 'tlc', powers south along the East Coast Main Line at Colton Junction on 7 December 2012, heading the Scottish Railway Preservation Society's 'Christmas Cracker' rail tour from Linlithgow near Edinburgh to Lincoln, for the Lincoln Christmas Market. West Coast Railways' Class 47 No 47851 brought up the rear.**

that were expected to bear fruit in 2013. The restoration of Sir Nigel Gresley's iconic 'A3' *Flying Scotsman*, bought by the NRM in 2004, continued in 'The Works'. Begun in 2006 and scheduled to take one year at a cost of about £75,000, this estimate was steadily increased to the region of £2.7 million, and still the work goes on. A recent report in the rail magazine *Steam Railway* noted that the loco's middle cylinder was misaligned and that the cost to the museum of carrying out the repairs could be as high as a further half a million pounds. In spite of these spiralling costs,

Two days later, on 9 December, the pairing of Nos 55022 and 47851 was to be seen again, this time passing Railway Cottages Crossing at Beningbrough, north of York, with train 5Z19, a Bo'ness to Carnforth loco movement, going via Castleton in Derbyshire to drop off the 'Deltic'. It looks like the 'Deltic' crew have their Christmas decorations up in the cab!

a spokeswoman for the NRM insisted, 'The National Railway Museum remains absolutely committed to the restoration of this iconic locomotive and to seeing it running once again on the British main line' (*The Press*, York, 7 January 2013).

Bringing York's Christmas 2012 steam festivities to a climax, two rail tours converged on the city on 22 December. First to appear was GWR 'Castle' No 5043 *Earl of Mount Edgcumbe*, which arrived on time at the head of train 1Z43 from Tyseley, 'The Christmas White Rose', to be welcomed at the station by 100 or so hardy enthusiasts who turned out in spite of the wet and cold conditions. About an hour later, and also running on time, came LNER 'A4' No 60009 *Union of South Africa* with train 1Z72, 'The Christmas Yorkshireman', from London Victoria.

What more has the great railway centre of York to give? Since the days of the steam era on BR this city has witnessed a transformation in its fortunes, seeing

'A3' 'Pacific' No 502 *Flying Scotsman* is seen from the viewing gallery of 'The Works' in the National Railway Museum, York, as her increasingly expensive restoration continued in December 2012.

Above and below: **GWR 'Castle' No 5043 *Earl of Mount Edgcumbe* arrives at York station with 'The Christmas White Rose', to be followed shortly afterwards by LNER 'A4' No 60009 *Union of South Africa* at the head of 'The Christmas Yorkshireman' on 22 December 2012.**

the closure of its once busy engine sheds, suffering the loss of the major employers the Wagon Works and the Carriage Works, and coping with the axing of railway lines to important parts of the region. At the same time the East Coast Main Line has been upgraded, signalling modernised, the world-renowned National Railway Museum established, and steam traction returned to our tracks on a regular basis. A major new Rail Operating Centre is under construction next to the station, capable of controlling train movements throughout much of the former Eastern Region, from London to Scotland. There are plans to upgrade the routes to Leeds and Harrogate, including electrification, and 2013 would see the reunion of all six surviving Gresley 'A4' streamlined 'Pacifics' at the NRM in York and later at Shildon.

What more has the great railway centre of York to give? Answer: much more!

13. 2013, the year of the 'A4' reunion for 'Mallard 75'

Above: **The commemorative plaque proudly carried by Sir Nigel Gresley's 'A4' No 4468 *Mallard*.**

Left: Mallard **herself waits within the Great Hall, while 'runners'** ***Bittern*, *Union of South Africa*** **and** ***Sir Nigel Gresley*** **were still operating on the main lines.**

To celebrate the 75th anniversary of *Mallard*'s record-breaking run, from 3 July 2013 the National Railway Museum in York hosted the 'once in a lifetime' reunion of the loco with her five surviving 'sisters'. The six locos were assembled together around the turntable in the Great Hall in an event entitled 'The Great Gathering', where for two weeks visitors could view *Mallard* with the other three UK-based streamliners, Nos 60007 *Sir Nigel Gresley*, 60009 *Union of South Africa* and 60019 *Bittern*, together with Nos 60008 *Dwight D. Eisenhower* and 60010 *Dominion of Canada*, both shipped across the Atlantic for this special occasion and having undergone cosmetic restoration in the NRM's workshops prior to the event.

By the final months of 2012 preparations were in an advanced state, with both of the exiled 'A4s' having been returned to the UK to be displayed alongside their four surviving classmates to honour No 4468 (BR 60022) *Mallard*

Gresley 'A4' No 60008 *Dwight D. Eisenhower* in 'The Works' at the NRM, York, on 12 December 2012, where she was being 'cosmetically restored' in preparation for 'Mallard 75' the following year. Sister loco No 60010 *Dominion of Canada* received similar attention at the NRM Shildon, but was repainted from her old and by now very tired-looking 'BR Green' to the striking 'Garter Blue' livery as carried in the 1930s, with the addition of the Canadian bell.

Above: **Near Copmanthorpe on the eastern approach to York, 'K4' No 61994 *The Great Marquess* runs 'topped and tailed' with 'K1' No 62005 on train 5Z62, a Bury (East Lancashire Railway) to York (NRM) loco move, on 29 March 2013.**

Right and below: **A second Easter loco move featured 'Black 5' Nos 44871 and 45407 *The Lancashire Fusilier*, travelling from Grosmont (North Yorkshire Moors Railway) to Shrewsbury (Severn Valley Railway), as train 5Z37 on 4 April. In the first picture No 44871 leads the way past Colton Junction, with sister loco No 45407 pushing the support coaches from the rear.**

achieving a speed of 126mph on 3 July 1938. The location of the achievement was Stoke Bank, south of Grantham, on the East Coast Main Line, where she set the world speed record for steam traction that still stands to this day. The six 'A4s' would be on display in York for a month, then at NRM Shildon during 2014, before the two North American locos returned across the Atlantic once more.

While this momentous event would undoubtedly grab the headlines in 2013, it was by no means the only attraction the great railway 'Mecca' of York had on offer during that year. Indeed, from the word 'go' the scene was set to build up to a climax in July.

Springtime in York is heralded by the sight of the banks of the City Walls outside the station coming alive, transformed into glorious yellow by the blooms of thousands of daffodils. It is at this time also that steam traction makes a welcome return, as heritage centres prepare for the coming season and locomotives are moved to new locations in advance of charter specials or on loan for the busy months ahead.

One of the unfortunate 'mishaps' of 2012 involved Stanier 8F No 48151 on 9 August,

All seems to be going smoothly as 8F No 48151 accelerates away from York towards Scarborough on 3 April 2013 with 'The Yorkshire Coast Express'.

when in charge of the ever-popular 'Scarborough Spa Express'. After causing lineside fires between York and the coast, she was removed and the tour completed with diesel haulage, prompting one observer to comment that the 8F had been 'trying to set fire to Yorkshire'. All was forgiven two weeks later when she was reinstated and completed the tour without further problems. A certain degree of apprehension was therefore understandable in the area when she appeared again on 3 April 2013, at the head of train 1Z94, 'The Yorkshire Coast Express', which had originated at Crewe and was steam-hauled from Carnforth to Scarborough by way of York. The outward leg ran smoothly, with No 48151 performing admirably and completing the journey on time and without cause for concern, but on her return trip the inevitable happened, and the frustrated Compass Tours passengers were halted at York following reports of fires along the track. The train was eventually rescued by a West Coast Railways Class 37, No 37516, sent from Carnforth, and got under way again after a delay of 4 hours, spent in Holgate Sidings. The offending 8F was left in the tender care of staff at the National Railway Museum.

Resplendent in 'BR Express Passenger Blue' livery, 'A1' No 60163 *Tornado* hurries south through Colton Junction towards London King's Cross with the returning 'Cathedrals Express' from York on 13 April 2013. *Rick Ward*

The National Railway Museum's preparations for the 'Mallard 75' celebrations included York's famous landmark, Clifford's Tower, being illuminated on the evening of Saturday 26 April with an art deco representation of the world's fastest steam locomotive to mark the start of the 75-day countdown.

Preserved diesels feature strongly among the stock of most heritage railways and springtime provides an ideal opportunity to show them off, often supplemented by 'guests' from other centres. In preparation for its Spring Diesel Gala over the weekend of 26-28 April 2013 the Keighley & Worth Valley Railway enlisted support from the North Yorkshire Moors Railway and the Bo'ness & Kinneil Railway in the shape of a quartet of preserved locos, moved in tow by West Coast Railways' Class 47 No 47786 *Roy Castle OBE*. Nos 20020, 26038, 37264 and D7628 are in convoy behind No 47786 near Colton, after having passed through York on 24 April on their way to the Worth Valley. *Rick Ward*

More changes to 'best laid plans' were needed for 'The Cathedrals Express' excursion of Saturday 13 April, operated by Steam Dreams, which had originally scheduled its King's Cross departure to travel to Scarborough and Durham, but due to 'pathing issues' near Doncaster the tour terminated at York. Nevertheless, entrusted into the capable hands of 'new-build' LNER Peppercorn Class 'A1' 'Pacific' No 60163 *Tornado*, all went well.

Passing the same location on 27 April is Class 57 No 57313 at the head of 1Z27, 'The Lakeland Moorlander', a West Coast Railways/Compass Tours excursion from Bishop Auckland to Carlisle and return, by way of York and the Settle and Carlisle line, with (out of shot) No 47854 on the rear. *Rick Ward*

Left and below: **The ever-popular 'Northern Belle' heads towards York on 27 April 2013, with a tour from Glasgow and Edinburgh to Harrogate (for the Spring Flower Show) and Harewood House. DRS Class 47 No 47501 *Craftsman* leads with No 47790 *Galloway Princess* at the rear as they pass close to Poppleton. *Both Rick Ward***

Steam power returned to York with a vengeance on Sunday 28 April 2013, offering a taste of things to come, when 'A4' Nos 60009 *Union of South Africa* and 4464 *Bittern* graced the metals with 'The Great Britain VI' rail tour.

By the end of May 2013 preparations for 'The Great Gathering' were well

Gresley 'A4' No 60009 *Union of South Africa* approaches York on 28 April 2013, bringing in the Edinburgh to York leg of 1Z28, 'The Great Britain VI', this being the final day of a nine-day tour, involving steam haulage from the Scottish capital to King's Cross. The arrival at York was unfortunately delayed by an hour due to a medical emergency near Durham.

Above: **The York to King's Cross leg, handled by sister loco No 4464 *Bittern*, more than made up the time after being rerouted along the ECML at Colton Junction instead of going via Gascoigne Wood as originally planned. Here No 4464 races south through Colton Junction.**

Left: **'A4' No 60009 *Union of South Africa* was in action again on 4 May, at the head of 1Z57, 'The Heart of Midlothian', hauling the York to Edinburgh section of a tour that had originated in Hull. She is seen here waiting at York station. *Rick Ward***

Below: **After leaving York 'No 9' accelerates past Shipton by Beningbrough and heads for the Scottish capital along the East Coast Main Line.**

advanced at the NRM. Nos 60008 *Dwight D. Eisenhower* and 4489 *Dominion of Canada*, both cosmetically restored by museum staff at York and Shildon respectively, took their places alongside No 4468 *Mallard* around the turntable in the Great Hall, having made their transatlantic voyage of more than 2,500 miles from North America the previous October. In a month's time they would be joined by their three remaining 'sisters' for the once-in-a-lifetime reunion.

Then, on 3 June 2013… Could the

unthinkable really happen? The timing of the announcement could hardly have been more dramatic. The news hit like a body blow that found its target without warning. Just one month before the long-awaited 'Mallard 75' celebrations, word came from the Director of the Science Museum Group (SMG), the National Railway Museum's parent organisation, that it was 'almost certain' that one of its three great northern museums would have to close, if Government funding cuts put a further squeeze on already overstretched budgets. The SMG runs the Museum of Science & Industry in Manchester, the National Media Museum in Bradford, and York's National Railway Museum, in addition to the Science Museum in London.

In an attempt to safeguard the NRM, York's local newspaper, *The Press*, launched a campaign and on-line petition, backed by tourism, political and business leaders as well as York Central MP Hugh Bayley and York Outer MP Julian Sturdy, aimed at rallying support for the threatened museum, which was hailed as one of York's biggest and most treasured attractions. A spokesman for the Department for Culture, Media & Sport was reported as commenting that it would be inappropriate at that time to speculate on the outcome of the Government's Spending Review, adding that 'this is an operational matter for the Science Museum Group who has to address a large projected operating deficit from 2014 onwards and it is assessing a range of options to address this situation.'

Cost-saving measures reportedly being

A most welcome return to York for LMS Stanier 'Pacific' No 46233 *Duchess of Sutherland* came when she headed 'The Yorkshire Coronation' rail tour operated by The Princess Royal Class Locomotive Trust (PMR Tours), and steam-hauled from Derby to Scarborough and return. No 46233 leans into the curve at Towthorpe on 11 May 2013. *Rick Ward*

explored included a reduced programme with scaled-down operational functions and the reintroduction of admission charges. Surely the internationally renowned and respected National Railway Museum could not seriously be a candidate for closure? George Stephenson

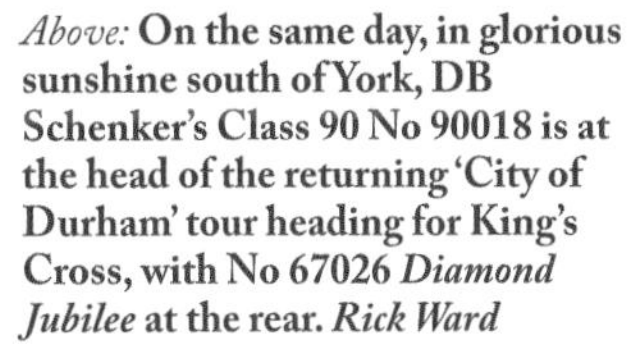

Above: **On the same day, in glorious sunshine south of York, DB Schenker's Class 90 No 90018 is at the head of the returning 'City of Durham' tour heading for King's Cross, with No 67026 *Diamond Jubilee* at the rear. *Rick Ward***

Left: **By May 2013 work on York's new Rail Operating Centre in the 'Engineer's Triangle' next to the station was well advanced, with the dimensions of this impressive facility plain to see. In the adjacent siding on the 23rd DRS Class 37 No 37423 *Spirit of the Lakes* is parked with Network Rail's Type 6B Buffet, Control Inspection Saloon No 975025 *Caroline*.**

Left and below: **Control Inspection Saloon *Caroline* and her nameplate.**

Approaching York at Colton Junction with a train of coal empties from one of the ever-hungry local power stations on 28 May 2013, pristine Class 66/7 No 66739, resplendent in blue with mustard-yellow cab livery and 'GB Railfreight, part of Europorte' branding, shows off her newly acquired nameplate. Now based at GBRf Peterborough, she emerged from General Motors EMD on 20 March 2005, was renumbered from 66579 on 30 June 2011, and named *Bluebell Railway* at the heritage line's Sheffield Park station on 28 March 2013. The naming ceremony was performed after she had brought in the first through train from London Victoria in 55 years, and was in recognition of the work performed by GBRf and its Class 66 locos in the clearing of landfill waste from Imberhorne Cutting, which facilitated the opening of the railway's Northern Extension connecting it once more to the national rail network at East Grinstead. Closed by BR in 1958 and reopened in 1960, this section of the former Lewes and East Grinstead line, dubbed the 'Bluebell Railway', thus became the first preserved standard-gauge steam-operated passenger railway in the world.

Above: Having travelled all the way from North America for the occasion, Gresley 'A4' Nos 4498 *Dominion of Canada* and 60008 *Dwight D. Eisenhower* grace the NRM's Great Hall on 4 June 2013.

Right: This statue of railway pioneer George Stephenson looks out over the Great Hall of the National Railway Museum in York.

Above: **'Then there were three', with No 4468 *Mallard* next to the turntable, awaiting the other three honoured guests for the big party starting on 3 July.**

would turn in his grave at such a prospect!

As calls for a formal debate in the House of Commons were voiced by York's MPs, a former head of the NRM, Andrew Dow, who was in charge between 1992 and 1994, suggested that it should become an independent museum, severing links with the Science Museum Group in order to act as a showcase for the railway industry, perhaps under the stewardship of a consortium consisting of (for example) Network Rail, the Association of Train Operating Companies and the freight companies. Mr Dow went on to comment that in this way 'it would be injected with a kind of understanding of railways that NRM seems to have lost while ever more space is given to eating facilities and retail outlets.' He concluded, 'There would be much to gain from returning the Museum to its roots, being of the industry and managed by the industry.'

The unfolding story was soon taken up by other newspapers across the region. *The*

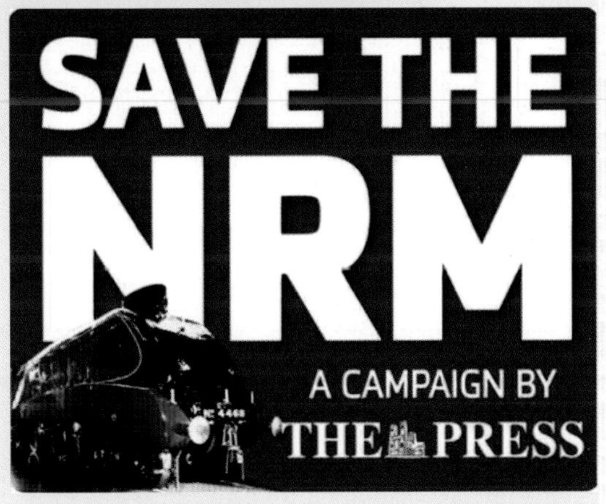

Northern Echo, with a circulation covering the Darlington, Durham and Middlesbrough areas, including the NRM's Shildon site, reflected on the resounding success of the York museum, reminding readers that it took the title of Museum of the Year in 1991 and European Museum of the Year 10 years later. The paper added that more than 200,000 visitors also passed through the doors of 'Locomotion' in Shildon, which itself had won numerous awards since its opening in 2004. Speculating that closure was thought to be 'highly unlikely', the reintroduction of entrance fees at York and Shildon was a distinct possibility, though its adverse effect on visitor numbers should not be underestimated.

The high-circulation *Yorkshire Post* reported that politicians from all parties across North and West Yorkshire were joining forces in the battle to save the threatened museums by fighting for a fair funding deal. York Outer Tory MP Julian Sturdy added that he would be lobbying Culture Minister Ed Vaizey on the matter.

Less than a week later, the *York Press* of Saturday 8 June weighed in with no fewer than three articles on the developing row over possible museum closures. The first, under the headline 'Council leaders question anti-North approach over museum threat', leaders of the Councils of the cities of York, Bradford and Manchester questioned why spending cuts might lead to one of their three museums facing closure, saying that this would be considered 'unthinkable' in London if applied to comparable national museums there such as the Victoria & Albert or the Natural History Museum.

A second piece, attributed to former NRM head Andrew Scott, who was in charge from 1994 until his retirement in 2010, argued that the Government's ban on admission charges for national museums should be relaxed if the expected funding cuts became a reality, while a third article in the same edition quoted an NRM spokeswoman as warning that the level of staffing might be an area where savings could be made, suggesting that the jobs of a number of 'explainers' could be lost as part of a cost-cutting drive.

The Archbishop of York, Dr John Sentamu, added his support to the campaign, saying that he was shocked to hear of the cuts that the three Northern museums were facing. He too felt that communities in the North seemed increasingly to be bearing the brunt of the economic downturn. Describing the NRM as 'one of the leading attractions in the whole country', he went on to argue that not only did it bring great enjoyment and pleasure to people across the age spectrum, but also contributed greatly to the wellbeing of the city and the local economy. 'We need to recognise that our cultural heritage is an important part of our country's history. A country which forgets its heritage becomes sterile,' he said.

At the same time, former Lord Mayor and train driver Bernard Bell voiced his feeling of disbelief at the news of the threat to the NRM, while within the city centre numerous shops supported the cause by displaying petition forms on their counters, and the on-line version launched by *The Press* attracted signatories in their thousands.

As momentum for the campaign to save the NRM grew daily, York Council leader James Alexander announced that a rally would be held outside the NRM on the lunchtime of Saturday 15 June, at which York Central MP Hugh Bailey would speak, stressing the national and international importance of the museum and urging the Science Museum Group to negotiate further with the Government in order to come to an amicable solution.

Following the rally, which was attended by about 100 banner-waving protesters, an open letter to the trustees of the Science Museum Group was sent jointly by the Councils of York, Bradford and Manchester, in which the economic and cultural impact of closing one of the threatened museums was described as 'devastating'. The following day brought a boost to hopes of saving the three museums, when Culture Minister Ed Vaizey suggested that the funding cuts proposed for museums would not be of the order of 10% as feared, but rather only 5% of their budgets, stating that 'they are not going to receive those level of cuts, so there is no reason why any of these museums should close'. York Outer MP Julian Sturdy welcomed the announcement, adding that the commitment expressed by the Minister to keeping the museums open would come as a relief not just to the people of York, but also to supporters across the country and indeed the world.

York Council leader James Alexander was more cautious, warning that while the Minister's assurances were encouraging, persistent pressing in support of these three nationally important Northern museums would continue until the Chancellor delivered confirmation in his revenue and capital statement. In the meantime, the 'Save the NRM' petition organised by the *York Press* continued to attract supporters, with more than 11,000 signatures.

On Friday 21 June, the 'Save the NRM' petition, by now signed by more than 12,500 people, was handed over to York's two MPs, who agreed to receive it jointly to signify all-party support for the campaign, and to present it to Government early the following week, before the Chancellor's crucial spending statement on Wednesday 26th.

On Monday 24th, the petition, now containing more than 13,500 signatures, was presented to the Government in the House of Commons by York Central MP Hugh Bayley. The following day a poll published by the world's largest travel website, Trip Advisor, listed the National Railway Museum in the top 25 museums in Europe and the 5th best in the UK, ahead of London's Victoria & Albert, Natural History and Imperial War museums.

Finally, on Tuesday 2 July, the Science Museum Group's director Ian Blatchford told MPs on the House of Commons Culture, Media & Sport select committee that, following the confirmation of the 5% cut in funding, rather than the 10% that had been feared, he was now in a position to give an assurance that none of the SMG's Northern museums would close. Responding to close questioning, Mr Blatchford confirmed that it had been the National Media Museum in Bradford that had been under greatest threat of closure. Following the meeting, City of York Council leader James Alexander welcomed the announcement and thanked everybody who had supported the campaign to secure the future of the nation's science museums, adding that he was 'delighted that the Government has listened to the powerful lobby ... and has agreed to work with us.'

Welcoming what he said could be 'a really significant breakthrough' from Culture Minister Ed Vaizey in the pursuit of a number of avenues of funding, Mr Blatchford concluded, 'No museum wanted to be a "subsidy junkie",' but, as the Minister said, 'The fury of the last three weeks has given us a wake-up call. While we have secured the future of these museums, no change is not an option.'

In York, after weeks of anxiety, one of the largest events in the National Railway Museum's history could now be celebrated and enjoyed by all, relieved of the burden that had threatened to overwhelm the unique occasion.

The year 2013 also marked the 75th anniversary of the outshopping of LMS Stanier 'Pacific' No 46233 *Duchess of Sutherland*. To mark the occasion, her owners, The Princess Royal Class Locomotive Trust, organised a two-day steam-hauled commemorative tour to Perth, 'The 75th Anniversary Special', including a gala dinner and hotel accommodation, on Friday 6 September, returning on the 7th. The

Stanier 'Duchess' 'Pacific' No 46233 *Duchess of Sutherland* races towards York near Beningbrough on Saturday 8 June with the return leg of 'The North Eastern', a tour originating at Derby and steam-hauled from Sheffield to Newcastle and back.

Right: **Confirming the attraction of York for railway enthusiasts, two further charters visited the city on that same day. Pathfinder Tours ran its 'York, Moors and Scarborough Explorer' train from Bristol Temple Meads, offering passengers a choice of venue for the afternoon, either visiting York, riding the North Yorkshire Moors Railway or spending time in the seaside resort. West Coast Railways provided the traction in the form of two of its preserved Class 47 diesels 'topping and tailing' the train. Not to be outdone, 'The Cumbrian Moorlander' arrived courtesy of Compass Tours. This train, also with West Coast Railways traction, involved a journey from Ayr to York and return, and is seen here with Class 57 No 57313 heading back to Scotland along the East Coast Main Line north of York, accompanied in the rear by Class 47 No 47760.**

Right and below: **A 'mid-week treat' on Tuesday 10 June 2013 was the visit to York of the A1 Steam Locomotive Trust's 'new-build' Peppercorn 'Pacific' No 60163 *Tornado*, hauling Pathfinder Tours' 1Z60 excursion from King's Cross to Edinburgh, 'The Elizabethan', re-enacting a scene from steam's glory days on the ECML. The tour, re-dated from Saturday 8 June, is seen in the first view passing the site of the former station at Shipton by Beningbrough, just north of York, and again behind preserved 'Deltic' No D9009 *Alycidon* on the evening's return leg, passing Railway Cottages Crossing north of Shipton.**

train ran from Crewe, where the loco was built, and travelled via the West Coast Main Line (where members of the class produced some of their outstanding runs during the glory days of steam) over Shap Summit to Carlisle. The loco then tackled the testing Beattock Bank to Glasgow, before continuing to her destination, the historic 'Fair City' of Perth, a journey of almost 300 miles.

Later in the year, on Saturday 12 October, 'The Duchess' was booked to head 'The Thames-Clyde Express' to Carlisle, by way of the mighty Settle and Carlisle line. This tour, originating at Lincoln, was steam-hauled by No 46233 from Hellifield to Carlisle and return.

Perhaps as a further 'taster' of events to come the following month, two of the main-line-certified Gresley 'A4s' graced the City of York with their presence on Friday 14 June. The occasion was the running of 'The Cathedrals Express to Scotland', a four-day tour from London King's Cross to Perth, organised by tour operator Steam Dreams. The first leg, to York, was handled by LNER No 4464 *Bittern*, resplendent in her blue livery, to be replaced by sister loco No 60009 *Union of South Africa* for the remainder of the run to Scotland. The tour then included two days north of the border with visits to Aberdeen and Inverness, before returning on Monday 17th, again steam-hauled.

As the final preparations were being made at the NRM for the 'Great Gathering', the last of the surviving former LNER 'A4s', No 4464 (aka 60019) *Bittern* made her appearance at the head of train 1Z 22, 'The Ebor Streak', on the morning of Saturday 29 June 2013. Having been given special permission by Network Rail to run up the ECML from King's Cross at up to 90mph (rather than the 75mph maximum normally allowed for preserved steam locomotives), *Bittern* passed Colton Junction 5 minutes early and arrived at a packed York station to be greeted by hundreds of steam fans who welcomed her back to what many consider to be her home.

As if the arrival of 'the last of the six' was not enough, enthusiasts were also treated, half an hour later, to the appearance of a star from 'the other side'. Former LMS 'Princess Coronation' 'Pacific' No 46233 *Duchess of Sutherland* graced the station hauling train 1Z 32, 'The Scarborough Flyer', from Tyseley to Scarborough and return.

LNER 'A4' No 4464 *Bittern* approaches York at Colton Junction with 1Z60, 'The Cathedrals Express' to Scotland, on Friday 14 June 2013.

Top: **Waiting at York was sister loco No 60009 *Union of South Africa*, ready to take the tour on to Edinburgh and Perth. She is seen here passing the site of the former station at Shipton by Beningbrough, a few miles north of York.**

Centre: **The returning 'Cathedrals Express' from Scotland arrived at the outskirts of York over an hour late on Monday 17 June, apparently caused by cattle having strayed onto the line further north, but by the time No 60009 passed Shipton it was clear that her crew intended to make up as much of the lost time as possible.**

Bottom: **The sense of urgency was still apparent after the change of engines at York, as No 4464 *Bittern* raced away past Copmanthorpe with the final leg of the four-day tour back to King's Cross. *Rick Ward***

Above: **'A4' No 4464 *Bittern* eases through Colton Junction on the approach to York, having topped 90mph further south at the head of 'The Ebor Streak' on 29 June 2013. Passengers would have the afternoon free to explore the city, while *Bittern* would be reunited with her surviving 'sisters' in preparation for the 'Mallard 75' event the following week.**

Right: **The return train in the evening was hauled by DB Schenker Class 90 electric locomotive No 90036, seen passing Copmanthorpe at the start of the journey back to King's Cross.**

Below: **'Princess Coronation' 'Pacific' No 46233 *Duchess of Sutherland* accelerates away from York on Saturday 29 June 2013, passing Towthorpe and heading for the coast with 'The Scarborough Flyer'.**

Mallard '75: 'The Great Gathering'
NRM, York, Wednesday 3 to Wednesday 17 July 2013

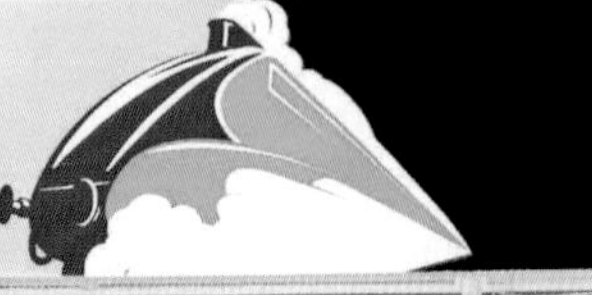

From left to right on 10 July are Nos 60007 *Sir Nigel Gresley*, 60008 *Dwight D. Eisenhower*, 60009 *Union of South Africa*, 4464 *Bittern*, 4468 *Mallard* and 4489 *Dominion of Canada*.

'The Great Gathering' at the NRM, with the six 'A4s' resplendent around the turntable in the Great Hall, attracted masses of visitors from far and wide. Many took advantage of the opportunity to travel by steam-hauled charter train to York, thus swelling the numbers thronging into the city for this unique occasion. Starting on Wednesday 3 July, the 75th anniversary of the famous world record run by *Mallard*, the event was opened by the record-breaker being propelled into the Great Hall and on to the turntable by the NRM's diesel shunter, No 09017, prominently carrying the logo of the sponsor 'Hornby' on its maroon livery. To the accompaniment of a musical fanfare, *Mallard* completed a 'lap of honour' on the turntable as her 'sisters' looked on in a semi-circle, before she took her place to complete the 'magnificent six' and the doors were opened to the public for the first time at 10.00am.

A record attendance at the museum was recorded on Saturday 6 July, with 12,000

Tour operator Steam Dreams brought its 'Cathedrals Express' tour to York from King's Cross to coincide with the opening day of the celebrations at the NRM in honour of Sir Nigel Gresley's 'A4' 'Pacific' *Mallard* setting the world record speed for steam traction of 126mph on that day 75 years before. Heading the returning train to King's Cross, 'A1' No 60163 *Tornado* passes Copmanthorpe on the outskirts of York. The passengers had joined the crowds thronging the NRM on the opening day of 'The Great Gathering', two weeks of celebrations to mark the 75th anniversary of *Mallard*'s record-breaking run.

Visitors enjoy the free show around the turntable in the Great Hall of the NRM. In the background are 'A4' Nos 60008 *Dwight D. Eisenhower* and 60009 *Union of South Africa*.

visitors passing through the doors, and nearly 45,000 being admitted over the first five days of 'The Great Gathering'.

Several steam-hauled specials added their passengers to the numbers visiting the event. On Wednesday 3 July came 'The Cathedrals Express' from London King's Cross, operated by Steam Dreams and hauled by 'A1' No 60163 *Tornado*. On Saturday 6th 'The Yorkshireman' arrived from London Victoria, operated by the Railway Touring Company and hauled by 'Britannia' Class No 70013 *Oliver Cromwell*. On the Sunday another 'Cathedrals Express' came from London King's Cross, operated by Steam Dreams and hauled once more by *Tornado*. On Saturday 13th the 'Coast to Coast Express' from Liverpool to Scarborough, operated by the Railway Touring Company (with the option for passengers to spend the afternoon in York), was hauled by 'Jubilee' Class No 45699 *Galatea*.

The NRM event continued until 17 July, to be followed by an 'Autumn Great Gathering' from 26 October to 6 November, when, as part of the annual 'Illuminating York' Festival, a competition entitled 'Locos in a Different Light' was held; students were able to illuminate the six 'A4s' with spectacular lighting to create unique photographic opportunities.

In addition, as part of the 75th anniversary celebrations, *Mallard* went 'on tour' along the East Coast Main Line during September 2013,

'A1' No 60163 *Tornado* accelerates away from York near Bolton Percy with the return leg of 'The Cathedrals Express' on 7 July 2013.

The star of the show, the record-breaker and still record-holder, *Mallard* herself, resplendent.

giving people in neighbouring regions the opportunity to see her first hand. Travelling first to Grantham, where the world speed record was set on Stoke Bank in 1938, she

With only 50 ticket-holders admitted for the early-morning photo-shoots, the line-up around the turntable could be admired unhindered.

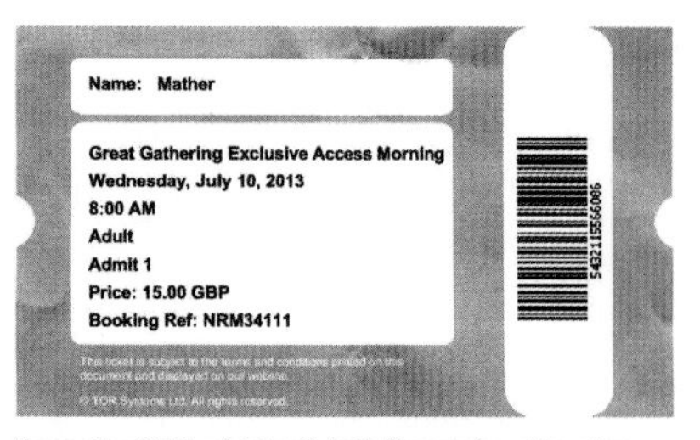
National Railway Museum

This is your ticket.
Please print and present on arrival.

Name: Mather

Great Gathering Exclusive Access Morning
Wednesday, July 10, 2013
8:00 AM
Adult
Admit 1
Price: 15.00 GBP
Booking Ref: NRM34111

5432115566086

You need to print this e-ticket and bring it with you to show at the entrance to the event. You need to print onto paper: we can't scan the ticket from a mobile phone screen.

By the time this momentous event ended after two weeks, during which the museum was the busiest it had ever been, 140,000 visitors had flocked in to see the 'famous six' around the turntable and be part of 'The Great Gathering'.

was the centrepiece of the 'Festival of Speed' exhibition, which also featured streamlined 1930s racing cars. Next she returned to Doncaster, her birthplace, for the annual St Leger Festival, where she was on display at Freightliner Ltd's Railport Depot on 14-15 September during a free event. Finally, *Mallard* joined other Doncaster-built locomotives to celebrate 160 years of Doncaster Works at the Barrow Hill Roundhouse in Chesterfield, Derbyshire, on 28-29 September.

Those enthusiasts willing to pay to avoid the 'madding crowd' were able to do so. For a pre-booked entrance fee of £15 per person, the NRM's doors were opened early for 2 hours from 8.00am, with entrance limited to 50 people on each day, giving the opportunity to photograph this special occasion in an uncrowded setting.

Finally, after more than a quarter of a million people visited the NRM at York during the 2013 celebrations, attention moved to the 'sister' museum at Shildon for 'The Great Goodbye' between 15 and 23 February 2014, which was the last chance to see the six together before the repatriated locos returned to their home museums during the summer of that year. As earlier at York, enthusiasts who were willing to pay and who booked early could avoid the crowds to enjoy the freedom of the two limited-access early-morning sessions, entitled 'Pacifics on Parade', though tickets for these were snapped up eagerly and many must have been disappointed.

When February arrived, the two North American 'A4s' were among the attractions at Barrow Hill Roundhouse, Staveley, near Chesterfield, over the weekend of the 8th and 9th, together with classmate *Bittern*, 'A1' No 60163 *Tornado*, 'A2' No 60532 *Blue Peter* together with 'Deltic' Nos D9009 *Alycidon* and 55019 *Royal Highland Fusilier*. The occasion, billed as 'East Coast Giants', was the last chance to see the repatriated 'A4s' before they were moved north by road for their final curtain-call at Shildon. On Wednesday 5th, the star of the show, *Mallard*, had been hauled up the East Coast Main Line from York by 'No 9' *Union of South Africa*. A few days later, on the

Heading for Shildon, 'A4' No 4464 *Bittern* passes Colton Junction on 11 February 2014. Perhaps anticipating a final happy reunion, she's running 20 minutes early at this point.

On 16 February, at NRM Shildon, the six 'A4s' are lined up for the early-morning photo-shoot and given a final dusting down before the admiring crowds are admitted.

The Great Goodbye
NRM Shildon
February 15th to 23rd 2014.
National Railway Museum

This is your ticket.
Please print and present on arrival.

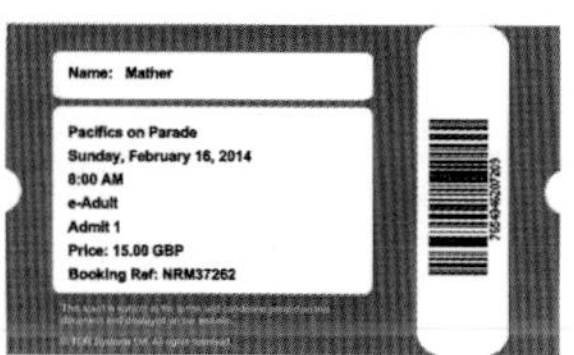
Name: Mather

Pacifics on Parade
Sunday, February 16, 2014
8:00 AM
e-Adult
Admit 1
Price: 15.00 GBP
Booking Ref: NRM37262

You need to print this e-ticket and bring it with you to show at the entrance to the event. You need to print onto paper: we can't scan the ticket from a mobile phone screen.

11th, 'No 19' (4464) *Bittern* made the journey from Barrow Hill (incidentally, as with *Union of South Africa*, in steam and with the same 'Identifier Code', 5Z28). The two North Americans, not being passed for rail running, made the journey up the A1 on

With No 60009 *Union of South Africa* between them, the two North American visitors pose in the morning sunshine. No 60008 *Dwight D. Eisenhower* (on the left) and No 4489 *Dominion of Canada* will soon leave Shildon and England, to head back across the Atlantic to their adopted homes. Safe journey!

The gates are open. Following the end of 'The Great Goodbye', the NRM announced that a record 119,800 'A4' fans had attended the museum at Shildon for this final event of the 'Mallard 75' programme.

low-loaders. To complete the reunion, 'No 7' *Sir Nigel Gresley* left home on the North Yorkshire Moors Railway at Grosmont on the 13th and, as 5Z31, also headed for Shildon. The scene was thus set for 'The Great Goodbye'.

Bibliography

BR Staff Association, 'The Railwayman's Year Book' (Railway Publications Ltd., 1957)

Burton, B. R. *York Carriage Works 1945-1995: The Final 50 Years of New Build* (1996)

Chapman, Stephen *Railway Memories No 24: Harrogate & Wetherby* (Bellcode Books, 2011)

Harris, Michael (ed) *This is York, Major Railway Centre* (Ian Allan, 1980)

Hoole, K. *The Railways of York* (Dalesman, 1976)

Hucknall, David *British Diesel Locomotives* (The History Press, 2010)

Myler, Chris *The Life and Times of York Carriage Works, 1884-1995* (ABB Rail/The Amadeus Press, 1996)

On Either Side (LNER Publications; Ben Johnson & Co, 1939)

Rose, Peter *Railway Memories No 5: Return to York* (Bellcode Books, 1994)

Ross, David *British Steam Railways* (Paragon, 2003)

Speakman, Colin *Transport in Yorkshire* (Dalesman, 1969)

Vaughan, John *Main Line Diesel Locomotives* (Haynes, 2011)

Index

Locations around York

Locomotive classes, diesel

Locomotive classes, electric

Locomotive classes, steam, pre-1968

GWR

LMS

LNER

SR

BR

Multiple units, diesel

York

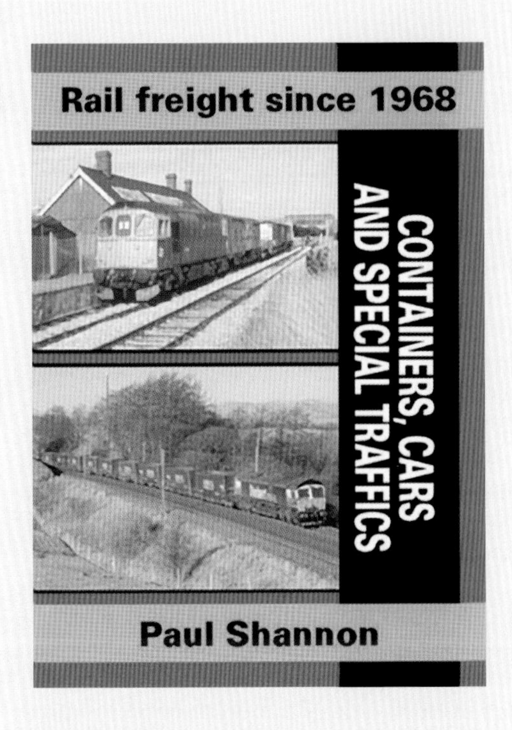

In this fourth and final volume in this popular series, Paul covers the remaining sectors of the Rail Freight business from 1968 to the present day.

The types of traffic covered include:

- Container traffic
- Charterail
- Channel Tunnel Intermodal
- Chemicals
- Nuclear traffic
- Milk
- Parcels, mail and newspapers

Using predominantly his own illustrations Paul examines in detail the changing scene. 1968 saw the end of steam on British Rail and this in itself had a massive impact on the operation of Britain's railways. Gone were the labour-intensive steam locomotive depots and many of the rural goods depots. In their place were new diesel and electric traction depots with a wide variety of locomotive types - cleaner to operate and more efficient to run. However, many were experimental in nature and breakdowns were not uncommon.

Gradually even the larger goods depots were being replaced with larger concentrated freight yards. New methods of handling the goods came in with the advent of containers designed to be used by rail, road and sea. Wagons were larger and carried higher and higher capacities, specialist loading and unloading facilities meant new traffic flows were needed as demand for movement by rail, having gone through a massive decline, began to recover, and the industry is seeing considerable growth potential going forward.

Size:	**238 x 172mm**
Extent:	**128pp**
Illustrations:	**c200 b&w**
ISBN:	**978 1 85794 347 4**
Format:	**Paperback**
RRP:	**£17.99**

In the same series

978 1 85794 263 7

978 1 85794 299 6

978 1 85794 264 4

Following the publication of the 1955 Modernisation Plan, which set out to establish the future of Britain's rail network, it seemed that the writing was on the wall for steam traction. With the Beeching Report the pace of change gathered speed, and the move to alternative traction was accompanied by considerable contraction of the network.

In the same series

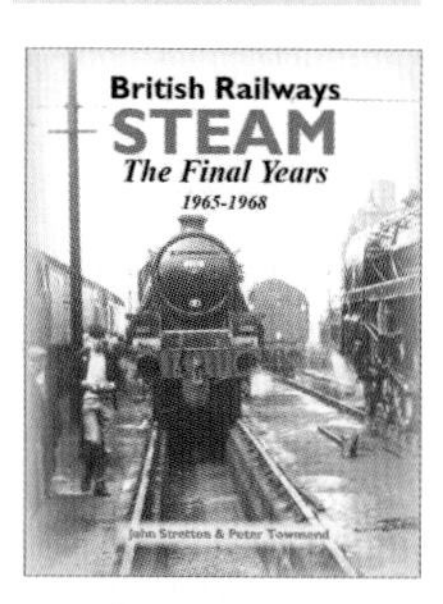

978 1 85794 320 7

The last steam locomotive built for British Railways, aptly named *Evening Star,* was outshopped from Swindon Works in 1960, and amazingly the last steam locomotives were withdrawn from service in August 1968! This decline from the mid-1950s forms the first part of this book, as hundreds upon hundreds of locomotives were sent to the breaker's yards. The scrap yards are the sombre location of the second section, which looks at these 'abattoirs of steam', where the vast majority of locomotives were despatched by the cutter's torch all too rapidly. However, among the scenes of devastation something remarkable was happening. Enthusiasts noticed that at one yard, old wagons were being cut up but locomotives were not. This was the remarkable yard of Dai Woodham at Barry Docks in South Wales – locomotives were going to Dai, but not to die!

Thanks in large part to this remarkable man we are able to move to our third section, the preservation years, when locomotives were reserved, then purchased (often gradually) and eventually moved to fledgling preserved lines all over the country to be restored. Having been banned seemingly for ever, steam eventually returned to the main line, and the book concludes with a look at today's thriving heritage railway scene, with more than 8 million visitors a year – a fall and rise indeed!

Size:	**276 x 213mm**
Extent:	**160pp**
Illustrations:	**c500 colour/b&w**
ISBN:	**978 1 85794 330 6**
Format:	**Hardback**
RRP:	**£30.00**

For further information on our range of titles:
Please visit our web site:
www.nostalgiacollection.com
from where our our latest catalogue is available